HUTCH

HUTCH

BASEBALL'S FRED HUTCHINSON AND A LEGACY OF COURAGE

WRITTEN BY MIKE SHANNON

ILLUSTRATED BY SCOTT HANNIG

McFarland & Company, Inc., Publishers
Jefferson, North Carolina, and London

Mike Shannon is also the author of the following books from McFarland

Baseball Books: A Collector's Guide (2008)

*Coming Back to Baseball: The Cincinnati Astros and
the Joys of Over-30 Play* (2005)

*Diamond Classics: Essays on 100 of the Best Baseball
Books Ever Published* (1989; paperback 2004)

*Everything Happens in Chillicothe: A Summer in the Frontier
League with Max McLeary, the One-Eyed Umpire* (2004)

*The Day Satchel Paige and the Pittsburgh Crawfords Came
to Hertford, N.C.: Baseball Stories and Poems* (1992)

LIBRARY OF CONGRESS CATALOGUING-IN-PUBLICATION DATA

Shannon, Mike.
Hutch : baseball's Fred Hutchinson and a legacy of courage /
written by Mike Shannon ; illustrated by Scott Hannig.
p.   cm.
Includes bibliographical references and index.

ISBN 978-0-7864-4625-4
softcover : 50# alkaline paper

1. Hutchinson, Fred, 1919–1964.   2. Baseball managers—
United States—Biography.   I. Title.
GV865.H87S43 2011   796.357092—dc22 [B]   2011009703

BRITISH LIBRARY CATALOGUING DATA ARE AVAILABLE

Cover illustration by Scott Hannig

Manufactured in the United States of America

*McFarland & Company, Inc., Publishers
Box 611, Jefferson, North Carolina 28640
www.mcfarlandpub.com*

FOR MY BEAUTIFUL WIFE TAMMY:
DESPITE THE FACT THAT I AM THE WAY I AM, YOU LOVE ME ANYWAY.

FOR MY CHILDREN JOE, WILL AND JULIA:
YOU CAN'T BEGIN TO KNOW HOW MUCH FUN IT IS BEING YOUR DAD.

FOR MY MOM:
YOU HAVE ALWAYS ENCOURAGED ME.

AND FOR THE MAN THAT I ADMIRE MOST, MY DAD, HANK HANNIG:
YOU HAVE ALWAYS BEEN MY HERO, POP.

—*Scott Hannig*

TO MY BEST FRIEND, MY DAD,
JOHN HUBERT SHANNON

—*Mike Shannon*

TABLE OF CONTENTS

PREFACE BY MIKE SHANNON

At a certain point every author becomes more keenly aware of the fact that the number of books he will be able to finish in his lifetime is finite. With this realization comes a determination to choose one's subjects even more wisely than ever before. This book is my 16th effort dedicated to baseball, and I couldn't have made a better choice in terms of the subject. Before I started the book, I knew a little about Fred Hutchinson, especially that an important baseball award had been named after him; but I suspected, correctly, that there was a great deal more to the story that was not commonly known, even by pretty knowledgeable fans, such as I style myself to be.

Without summarizing the book here, suffice it to say that I learned that Fred Hutchinson was involved in far more important baseball events and storylines than I even imagined or hoped for. These I leave you to discover for yourself in the following pages. More importantly, my respect and admiration for Hutch grew by leaps and bounds as I followed in his footsteps, and I am certain that you will feel the same way towards this great baseball man and person after you have finished reading his story.

Another fortuitous decision represented by the book in your hands was the choice of Scott Hannig as the artist. No graphic novel author could ever hope for a better collaborator. The realistic yet nostalgic look of Scott's drawings was perfect for the tone of the book; and no matter what person, action, or idea I gave him to illustrate, he was always up to the challenge. There are at least 803 distinct images of his in the book, and every one of them is a work of art. In addition, Scott maintained a determination to make the book and his drawings as historically accurate as possible. He was never satisfied to settle for something generic or imagined when more research might provide a specific, historical detail. Careful readers may detect numerous instances of such details, which are due to Scott's tenacity. To say that this book was a labor of love for Scott, a lifelong Cincinnati Reds fan, is both accurate and an understatement. It would be closer to the truth to say that it was an obsession. He spent many many grueling but enraptured hours away from his lovely family (wife Tammy and kids Joe, William, and Julia) while working on the book, and for this dedication I am grateful beyond words.

As always, there are a number of other people to thank now that the book is finished, and Scott and I would like to acknowledge the help of Brent Hannig, Philip Schwartz, Christi Loso of the Fred Hutchinson Cancer Research Center, Bryce Covey of Team Photogenic, Anne Jewell of the Louisville Slugger Museum, Chris Eckes of the Cincinnati Reds Hall of

1

Fame; David Eskenazi, an expert on professional baseball in the Northwest; and Joe Helm, who lent us a newspaper scrapbook he'd kept of the 1961 Reds season. Special thanks must go to good friend and business partner Tom Eckel, who lent me numerous volumes from his collection of The Sporting News which were invaluable to my research. Finally, I am blessed with a large and loving family, and for their constant interest and encouragement I thank my father John H. Shannon, my aunt Jane Shannon, my sister Laura Smiley and her husband Jeff, my sister Susie Klemmt and her husband Lyle, my bother John and his wife Janice, my brother Tim and his wife Carla, my nephews Andrew Smiley, John Marcel Shannon, and Riley Shannon, and my nieces Rachel and Laura Shannon. Most of all, I am grateful for the love and support of my beautiful wife, Kathleen A. Dermody, who made my life when she married me, and for that of my five children, of whom I am so proud: Meghann Shannon, Casey Schneider (and her husband Keith), Mickey Shannon, Bridget Al-Atat (and her husband Hassan), and Nolan Ryan Shannon.

Ad majorem Dei gloriam.

CHAPTER 1

**The Pride
of Seattle,
1919–1938**

"The ones who work the hardest are the ones who make it, the ones who win. Sometimes that's the only difference. If you don't work hard at this game, you might as well hang them up. Sweat is your only salvation."

Fred Hutchinson as told to Emmett Watson, Hutch's high school catcher who became Seattle's preeminent newspaper columnist.

IN THE SUMMER OF 1919 CHAMPAGNE WAS
FLOWING IN CINCINNATI'S FAMOUS FOUNTAIN.①

... OR SO IT SEEMED TO THE FANATICS WHO CROWDED INTO REDLAND FIELD.

LED BY CENTERFIELDER EDD ROUSH AND THIRD BASEMAN HEINIE GROH THE REDS WERE ON THEIR WAY TO THE CITY'S 1ST NATIONAL LEAGUE CHAMPIONSHIP.

STANDING IN THEIR WAY: THE BAD-ASS N.Y. GIANTS...

... AND THEIR LEGENDARY MANAGER, JOHN McGRAW, BASEBALL'S LITTLE NAPOLEON.

The New York Times

CRUCIAL SERIES AT THE POLO GROUNDS
GIANTS HOST UPSTART REDS IN
3 STRAIGHT DOUBLE-HEADERS

ON AUGUST 13, THE REDS MARCHED INTO NEW YORK WITH A 4½ GAME LEAD OVER THE GIANTS

THE REDS SWEPT THE FIRST DOUBLEHEADER 4-3 AND 2-1.

THE NEXT DAY THE GIANTS WON A PAIR 2-1 AND 9-3.

A CINCINNATI SWEEP OF THE FINAL TWIN BILL BOOSTED THE REDS' LEAD TO 6½ GAMES, AND PAT MORAN'S BOYS WERE NOT SERIOUSLY CHALLENGED AGAIN THAT SEASON.

THE REDS FINISHED THE SEASON WITH A STERLING 96–44 RECORD AND BOASTED
A TRIO OF PITCHING ACES WITH DUTCH RUETHER, SLIM SALLE, AND HOD ELLER.②

THEY WON 8 MORE GAMES THAN THEIR AMERICAN LEAGUE COUNTERPARTS,
YET THE MORE FAMOUS AND MORE EXPERIENCED CHICAGO WHITE
SOX WERE WIDELY EXPECTED TO WIN THE WORLD SERIES.③

WHEN THE BETTING ODDS SUDDENLY
SHIFTED DRAMATICALLY IN FAVOR OF
THE REDS, RUMORS BEGAN TO SWIRL
THAT THE WORLD SERIES WAS FIXED.④

SOME OF THE WHITE SOX WERE ANGRY WITH TEAM OWNER CHARLES COMISKEY.(5)

THEY FELT UNDERPAID AND UNAPPRECIATED.(6)

AND SO THEY DID ACCEPT PAYOFFS FROM GAMBLERS.(7)

WHEN THE REDS' LEADOFF BATTER IN THE SERIES WAS PLUNKED IN THE BACK, INSIDERS KNEW THAT THE FIX WAS IN.(8)

UNCHARACTERISTICALLY LACKLUSTER PITCHING AND SUSPICIOUS ERRORS BY THE SOX HELPED THE REDS TAKE A 4 GAMES TO 1 LEAD IN THE BEST-OF-NINE SERIES.(9)

THE GAMBLERS PLAYED THE WHITE SOX FOR SUCKERS AND DELIVERED ONLY A PORTION OF THE PROMISED AMOUNT.

IN RETALIATION, THE WHITE SOX DOUBLE-CROSSED THE GAMBLERS AND TOOK GAMES 6 AND 7.[10]

THE ODDS THEN SHIFTED BACK TO CHICAGO AS THE WHITE SOX'S REVERSION TO FORM CAUSED MANY FANS TO BET ON THEM TO WIN THE SERIES.

THE GAMBLERS REGAINED CONTROL BY HAVING A THUG THREATEN TO HARM THE WIFE OF LEFTY WILLIAMS, THE SOX'S PITCHER SCHEDULED TO START GAME 8.[11]

THE SCARE TACTIC WORKED. WILLIAMS GAVE UP 4 RUNS IN THE 1ST INNING, AND THE REDS CRUISED TO A 10–5 WIN, CAPTURING THE 1ST WORLD CHAMPIONSHIP IN TEAM HISTORY.[12]

THE UGLY, NEVER-ENDING RUMORS LED TO AN INVESTIGATION AND TRIAL THE FOLLOWING YEAR.[13]

DESPITE THE "NOT GUILTY" VERDICT OF THE JURY, COMMISSIONER KENESAW MOUNTAIN LANDIS ISSUED A LIFETIME BAN FROM PROFESSIONAL BASEBALL TO THE 8 CHICAGO PLAYERS WHO HAD PARTICIPATED IN OR KNOWN ABOUT THE FIX.[14]

THE BANNED PLAYERS BECAME KNOWN AS THE BLACK SOX.

BUCK WEAVER   JOE JACKSON   OSCAR FELSCH   EDDIE CICOTTE

THEIR DISHONESTY TAINTED THE TRIUMPH OF THE REDS AND
SHOOK THE PUBLIC'S CONFIDENCE IN THE GAME.⑮

CLAUDE WILLIAMS   CHICK GANDIL   SWEDE RISBERG   FRED McMULLIN

FORTUNATELY, THE GAME'S GREATEST HERO TOOK
CENTER STAGE TO HELP MAKE THINGS RIGHT.⑯

AND EVEN DURING THAT SUMMER
RIGHT BEFORE BASEBALL'S DARKEST
HOUR, THERE WAS BORN IN SEATTLE,
WASHINGTON, ANOTHER WHO WOULD
TREAT THE GAME RESPECTFULLY
AND WITH GREAT COURAGE BRING
HONOR TO IT IN CINCINNATI.

BORN AUGUST 12, 1919, FREDERICK CHARLES HUTCHINSON WAS THE THIRD SON OF DR. JOSEPH LAMBERT AND NONA HUTCHINSON.

FRED'S PARENTS WERE BOTH FROM WISCONSIN.[17]

THEY SETTLED IN THE RAINIER BEACH AREA OF SE SEATTLE WHERE DR. HUTCHINSON WENT INTO BUSINESS AS A GENERAL PRACTITIONER.

BOTH OF FRED'S OLDER BROTHERS WERE CRAZY ABOUT BASEBALL AND GOOD ENOUGH TO PLAY AT THE UNIVERSITY OF WASHINGTON FOR REVERED COACH DORRETT "TUBBY" GRAVES.[18]

WHILE AT UW, JOHN HUTCHINSON ATTRACTED THE ATTENTION OF THE PROS AND EVEN PLAYED A SUMMER IN THE ST. LOUIS BROWNS' ORGANIZATION.

BILL HUTCHINSON, A 3RD BASEMAN, CAPTAINED THE HUSKIES AND BATTED .410 HIS SENIOR YEAR.

BILL SIGNED A CONTRACT WITH THE MINOR LEAGUE SF MISSIONS AND WAS INVITED BY THE PITTSBURGH PIRATES TO ATTEND SPRING TRAINING.

BUT BILL DECIDED TO FOLLOW IN HIS FATHER'S FOOTSTEPS.

AFTER GRADUATING FROM UW, HE ENROLLED IN THE McGILL UNIVERSITY MEDICAL SCHOOL...

...AND LATER DID HIS INTERNSHIP AND SURGERY RESIDENCY AT BALTIMORE UNION MEMORIAL HOSPITAL.

BILL MARRIED A SURGICAL NURSE HE HAD MET IN BALTIMORE...

...AND TOGETHER THEY MOVED TO SEATTLE WHERE BILL BECAME A SUCCESSFUL SURGEON. [19]

BILL AND CHARLOTTE (NÉE RIGDON) WERE LATER BLESSED WITH FIVE CHILDREN.

HOWEVER, LONG BEFORE HIS OWN CHILDREN CAME ALONG BILL PERFECT- ED HIS PARENTING SKILLS BY SERVING AS A GREAT BIG BROTHER TO FRED. [20]

BILL AND JOHN BOTH SPENT HOURS UPON HOURS TEACHING BASEBALL TO THEIR YOUNGER BROTHER WHO SOAKED UP THEIR LESSONS LIKE A SPONGE. [21]

HIS BROTHERS MADE FRED A LEFT-HANDED HITTER SO HE'D HAVE AN ADVANTAGE RUNNING TO 1ST BASE.

THEY MADE HIM A CATCHER BECAUSE HE WAS A BIG TOUGH KID WITH HUGE HANDS AND A GOOD ARM.

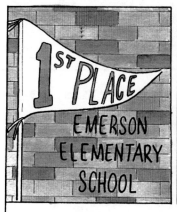

AS A CATCHER FRED LED EMERSON AND BRIGHTON ELEMENTARY SCHOOLS TO CITY CHAMPIONSHIPS.

BY THE TIME HE ENTERED HIGH SCHOOL FRED WAS ALREADY A WELL KNOWN ATHLETE IN SEATTLE.

IN HIS SOPHOMORE YEAR FRED CLIMBED ATOP THE MOUND AND QUICKLY BECAME THE ACE OF THE SCHOOL'S PITCHING STAFF.

HIS HITTING WAS SO LUSTY THAT HE CONTINUED TO CATCH OR PLAY 1ST BASE OR THE OUTFIELD WHEN HE WASN'T PITCHING.

WITH FRED AS THE TEAM STAR, FRANKLIN HIGH WON 4 STRAIGHT SEATTLE CITY CHAMPIONSHIPS.

DURING THE SUMMERS FRED ALSO PLAYED FOR AMERICAN LEGION TEAMS COACHED BY HIS HIGH SCHOOL COACH, AND HE RARELY LOST A GAME HE PITCHED.[22]

FRED WAS NOT THE FASTEST PITCHER AROUND, BUT THE BIG RIGHT-HANDER HAD GREAT CONTROL...

...AND HE WAS A STEELY COMPETITOR.

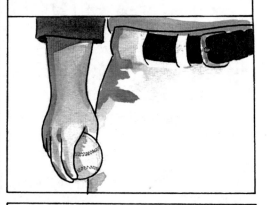

SCOUTS FROM 4 DIFFERENT MAJOR LEAGUE CLUBS WERE ON HAND TO WATCH THE FIRST GAME OF FRED'S SENIOR YEAR.[23]

UNDISTRACTED BY THE ATTENTION, FRED STRUCK OUT 18 BATTERS WHILE PITCHING A ONE-HITTER.

16

THE SCOUTS WERE NOT IMPRESSED THOUGH AND THOUGHT THAT FRED'S "NOTHING" BALL WOULD BE HIT BY BETTER COMPETITION.

SCHOOL BOYS CERTAINLY NEVER FIGURED OUT FRED. HE LOST ONE GAME AS A HIGH SCHOOL PITCHER.

THE MAJOR LEAGUE CLUB MOST INTERESTED IN FRED WAS THE DETROIT TIGERS.

HOWEVER, THEY BALKED AT THE $5,000 SIGNING BONUS FRED'S FATHER THOUGHT HIS SON DESERVED.

UNDETERRED, FRED PITCHED FOR THE
SEMI-PRO YAKIMA INDIANS IN 1937.

HE WAS PAID $20 A GAME AND WON
16 OF 18 DECISIONS.

THE FOLLOWING YEAR HE SIGNED
A CONTRACT TO PITCH FOR THE
HOMETOWN SEATTLE RAINIERS.

THE RAINIERS WERE MEMBERS
OF THE PACIFIC COAST LEAGUE,
THE P.C.L. FOR SHORT.

P.C.L. TEAMS WERE LOCATED ALONG THE
WEST COAST AND INCLUDED PORTLAND, LOS
ANGELES, HOLLYWOOD, SACRAMENTO, SAN
FRANCISCO, OAKLAND, AND SAN DIEGO.

THE AA P.C.L. WAS JUST A STEP BELOW THE BIG LEAGUES...

...AND MANY OF THE LEAGUE'S BEST PLAYERS, SUCH AS JOE DIMAGGIO, OFTEN WENT ON TO BECOME STARS IN THE MAJORS.㉔

LIFE

JOE DIMAGGIO

MAY 1, 1939 10 CENTS

IN 1938 THE RAINIERS HELD SPRING TRAINING IN EL CENTRO, CALIFORNIA.

"HUTCH," AS THE PLAYERS CALLED YOUNG FRED, IMMEDIATELY IMPRESSED EVERY-ONE WITH HIS POISE AND FEARLESSNESS.

BACK IN SEATTLE, NEWSPAPERS DESCRIBED HIM AS "THE SENSATION OF TRAINING CAMP."

WHEN THE 1938 SEASON OPENED, FRED HUTCHINSON WAS IN UNIFORM, A PROFESSIONAL BALLPLAYER AT AGE 18.

MANAGER JACK LELIVELT HAD A LOT OF CONFIDENCE IN HUTCH...[25]

...AND HE SHOWED IT BY STARTING THE YOUNGSTER IN THE 2ND GAME OF THE SEASON AGAINST THE S.D. PADRES.

UNDERSTANDABLY, HUTCH WAS NERVOUS IN HIS PROFESSIONAL DEBUT.

HE LASTED 1 INNING, GIVING UP 2 RUNS ON 2 HITS AND 3 BASES ON BALLS.

HUTCH SHED A FEW TEARS OF DISAPPOINTMENT BUT VOWED TO DO BETTER NEXT TIME.

AND DO BETTER HE DID IN A 2—1 WIN OVER OAKLAND IN HIS 2ND START.

ALTHOUGH NOT CREDITED FOR THE WIN AGAINST THE OAKS, HUTCH WON HIS NEXT 5 OUTINGS.

THE PRESS IN SEATTLE DUBBED HIM "THE ICEMAN" FOR HIS COOLNESS UNDER FIRE.

ON JUNE 15 THE RAINIERS PLAYED THEIR 1ST GAME
IN THEIR NEW CONCRETE AND STEEL BALLPARK.[26]

THE BALLPARK WAS NAMED AFTER
THE TEAM'S OWNER, EMIL G. SICK,
A WEALTHY BREWER WHO HAD
BOUGHT THE BANKRUPT FRANCHISE
THE YEAR BEFORE.

THE PARK WAS LOCATED IN RAINIER
VALLEY, AND MAJESTIC MOUNT RAINIER
LOOMED ABOVE THE GRANDSTAND.

TWELVE THOUSAND FANS WERE ON HAND
TO INAUGURATE SICK'S STADIUM, BUT THE
RAINIERS LOST TO PORTLAND, 3-1.

SEATTLE GOT WIN #1 IN THEIR NEW DIGS THE NEXT DAY WHEN HUTCH SHUT OUT THE BEAVERS, 7-0.

THE RAINIERS' YOUNG STUD WAS THE TALK OF BASEBALL, AND FRED BEGAN TO DRAW CROWDS OF 10,000+ WHENEVER HE PITCHED.

NO ONE COULD BELIEVE THE 18-YEAR-OLD'S COMPOSURE.

HUTCH PSYCHED OUT THE OPPOSITION IN WAYS THAT WOULD HAVE MADE SATCHEL PAIGE PROUD.

LATER THAT SUMMER THE BEAVERS SEEMED TO HAVE HUTCH ON THE ROPES.

23

NURSING A 5–2 LEAD IN THE 8TH INNING, HUTCH FELL BEHIND IN THE COUNT 2–0.

TO THE ASTONISHMENT OF ALL, THE BRASH KID CALLED "TIME," AND THEN WALKED SLOWLY TO THE DUGOUT.

WITH FEARED SLUGGER HARRY ROSENBERG CHAFFING AT THE DELAY, HUTCH TOOK A SERIES OF DRINKS FROM THE WATER FOUNTAIN.

HE SAT DOWN AND APPLIED A WET TOWEL TO HIS FOREHEAD.

REFRESHED AND RELAXED, HUTCH RETIRED THE IMPATIENT AND IRRITATED ROSENBERG, AS WELL AS THE NEXT 2 BATTERS, TO END THE INNING WITHOUT ANY SCORING.

AFTER THE RAINIERS' WIN, HUTCH EXPLAINED: "IT WAS A HOT DAY OUT THERE."

ON AUGUST 12 AN OVERFLOW CROWD OF 16,000
JAMMED INTO SICK'S STADIUM TO WATCH FRED PITCH...

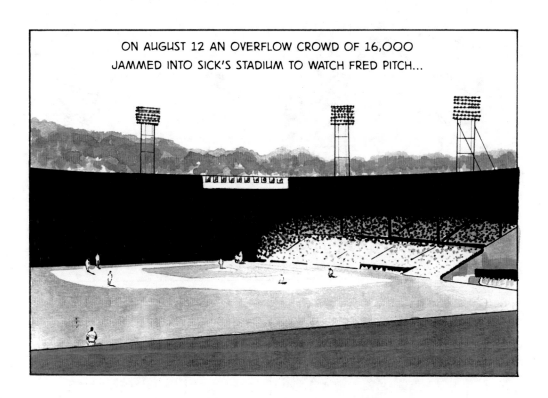

...AND TO CELEBRATE HIS 19TH BIRTHDAY.

HUTCH BEAT SAN FRANCISCO 3-2 FOR
HIS 19TH WIN OF THE SEASON!

25

FIVE DAYS LATER HUTCH WON HIS 20TH GAME WITH A 9-0 SHUTOUT OF SACRAMENTO.

FRED'S HITTING WAS AS GOOD AS HIS PITCHING. HE WALKED ONCE, BANGED OUT 2 SINGLES...

...AND DROVE A PITCH OVER THE RF WALL FOR A HOME RUN.

"THE GREATEST ONE-MAN EXHIBITION I'VE EVER SEEN IN ALL MY YEARS IN BASEBALL."

RAINIERS MANAGER JACK LELIVELT

THE HITS WERE NO FLUKE, AS HUTCH FINISHED THE SEASON WITH THE HIGHEST BATTING AVERAGE (.313) ON THE TEAM.

THROUGHOUT SEPTEMBER THE RAINIERS BATTLED LOS ANGELES AND SACRAMENTO FOR THE P.C.L. CHAMPIONSHIP.㉗

L.A. FINALLY WON THE PENNANT, BUT SEATTLE'S RUNNER-UP FINISH AND 100–75 RECORD WAS A VAST IMPROVEMENT.

FOR THIS TURN-AROUND HUTCH AND 4 TEAMMATES WERE NAMED TO THE P.C.L. ALL-STAR TEAM.

IN RECOGNITION OF HIS 25–7 RECORD AND 2.48 ERA (IN 290 INNINGS) HUTCH WAS VOTED THE MVP OF THE P.C.L....

...AND NAMED THE MINOR LEAGUE PLAYER OF THE YEAR BY *THE SPORTING NEWS*.

FRED WAS NOW THE HOTTEST PROSPECT IN BASEBALL...WORTH, SOME SPECULATED, $100,000.[28]

DETROIT NO LONGER HAD ANY DOUBTS ABOUT HUTCH, AND IN DECEMBER THEY PURCHASED HIM FROM SEATTLE FOR $50,000 AND 4 PLAYERS.[29]

Jo-Jo White   George Archie   Tony Piet   Ed Selway

THE DEAL HELPED THE RAINIERS WIN THE NEXT 2 P.C.L. PENNANTS, AND DUE TO A CLAUSE IN HUTCH'S SEATTLE CONTRACT...

...IT FINALLY PUT A $5,000 DETROIT BONUS INTO HIS POCKET![30]

CHAPTER 2

Major League Pitcher, 1939–1952

*"Fred Hutchinson stands as a mockery of
the statement that 'Nice guys finish last.'"*

Detroit sportswriter Watson Spoelstra

FRED'S NEW HOME WAS BRIGGS STADIUM. BUILT IN 1912 THE
INTIMATE BALLYARD HAD ALREADY HOSTED 2 WORLD SERIES.[1]

BECAUSE DETROIT'S VETERANS DID ALL THE PITCHING, THE HERALDED
ROOKIE SPENT THE EARLY PART OF THE SEASON SITTING AND WATCHING.[2]

FRED FINALLY MADE HIS MAJOR LEAGUE DEBUT ON MAY 2, 1939, IN A GAME DESTINED TO BE FAMOUS FOR WHO DID NOT PLAY IN IT.

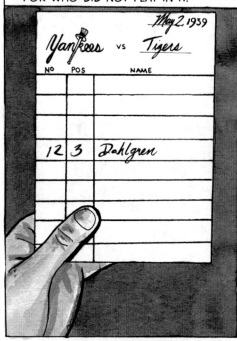

May 2, 1939

Yankees VS Tigers

NO	POS	NAME
12	3	Dahlgren

FOR YEARS LOU GEHRIG HAD TEAMED WITH BABE RUTH TO GIVE THE NEW YORK YANKEES THE MOST POWERFUL AND TERRIFYING ONE-TWO BATTING PUNCH IN HISTORY.

BUT NOW GEHRIG WAS DYING FROM A TERRIBLE DISEASE THAT WOULD ONE DAY BEAR HIS NAME. AS GEHRIG HANDED THE YANKEES' LINEUP CARD TO THE UMPIRE, THE CROWD CHEERED IN RESPECT AND ADMIRATION.[3]

AFTER PLAYING IN 2,134 CONSECUTIVE GAMES, THE IRON
HORSE STOOD ASIDE FOR A YOUNGER, HEALTHIER PLAYER.
HE CHEERED HIS TEAMMATES ON FROM THE DUGOUT AND
NEVER APPEARED IN A MAJOR LEAGUE GAME AGAIN.④

EVEN GEHRIG-LESS THE YANKEES STILL HAD PLENTY OF BIG BATS.⑤ THEY POUNDED OUT 17 HITS, INCLUDING FOUR HOME RUNS...

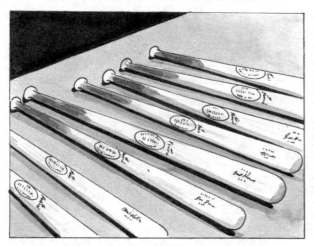

...AND TROUNCED DETROIT 22-2.

HUTCH ENTERED THE GAME IN THE 7TH INNING, THE 4TH TIGERS PITCHER OF THE DAY.⑥

BUT HE TOO WAS KNOCKED OUT OF THE BOX AFTER GIVING UP 4 HITS IN $2/3$ OF AN INNING.

TO GET FRED THE WORK HE NEEDED, DETROIT SENT HIM DOWN TO THEIR FARM TEAM IN TOLEDO, OHIO.

FRED'S 9-9 RECORD WAS THE BEST ON THE TEAM. IT EARNED HIM A SPOT ON THE A.A. ALL-STAR TEAM...AND A CALL-UP BACK TO DETROIT.

Toledo to Detroit

34

ON JULY 25 FRED MADE HIS 1ST MAJOR LEAGUE START BUT LOST TO THE SENATORS IN WASHINGTON 5-3.⑦

FIVE DAYS LATER HE NOTCHED HIS 1ST MAJOR LEAGUE WIN, OVER THE PHILADELPHIA A'S IN SHIBE PARK.⑧

HUTCH PICKED UP HIS SECOND WIN AUGUST 6, BEATING TED WILLIAMS AND THE RED SOX IN BOSTON, 10-1.⑨

A 17-3 SPANKING BY THE LOWLY ST. LOUIS BROWNS BROUGHT FRED BACK DOWN TO EARTH THOUGH,... ⑩

...AND INCONSISTENCY, WILDNESS, AND FRESHMAN MISTAKES HAMPERED HIS EFFORTS THE REST OF THE YEAR. HE WAS HARDLY SATISFIED WITH HIS ROOKIE SEASON AND LEFT DETROIT DETERMINED TO DO BETTER IN 1940.⑪

AFTER A BIT OF A SLIP IN 1939, THE
TIGERS AND THEIR FANS WERE PRIMED
FOR A RUN AT THE 1940 A.L. PENNANT.[12]

A FAST START ELUDED FRED THOUGH,
AND AFTER HE LOST HIS FIRST 2 STARTS
HE WAS RETURNED TO THE MINORS FOR
MORE SEASONING.[13]

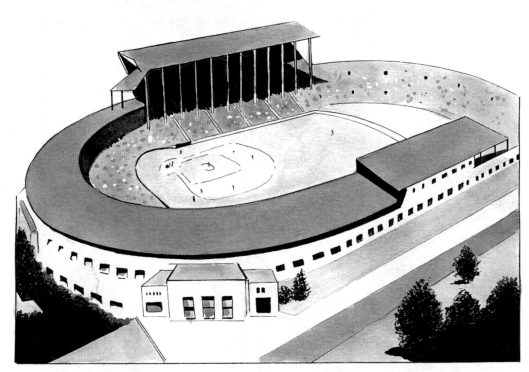

IN BUFFALO FRED REGAINED HIS OLD DAZZLING FORM. HE WENT 7-3 IN
94 INNINGS, AND HIS 2.49 ERA WAS 3RD BEST IN THE INTERNATIONAL LEAGUE.
HE WAS RECALLED TO THE MOTOR CITY IN JULY. EVERY ONE OF HIS SUBSEQUENT
3 VICTORIES WAS IMPORTANT AS THE TIGERS WITH THEIR 90-64 RECORD EDGED
OUT THE CLEVELAND INDIANS FOR THE PENNANT BY A SINGLE GAME.[14]

Hank Greenburg

Rudy York

Barney McCoskey

THE TIGERS' FEARSOME LINEUP WAS ANCHORED BY A PAIR OF SLUGGERS, HANK GREENBERG (.340, 41, 151) AND RUDY YORK (.316, 33, 134); AND BOLSTERED BY OTHER TALENTED BATSMEN, SUCH AS OUTFIELDERS BARNEY McCOSKEY (.340) AND 2ND BASEMAN CHARLIE GEHRINGER (.313). ECCENTRIC BOBO NEWSOM (21–5) SERVED AS THE ACE OF THE PITCHING STAFF AND WAS ABLY BACKED UP BY SCHOOLBOY ROWE (16–3), TOMMY BRIDGES (12–9), AND HAL NEWHOUSER (9–9).

Charlie Gehringer

Bobo Newsom

Schoolboy Rowe

Bucky Walters

Paul Derringer

Joe Beggs

THE TIGERS' OPPONENTS IN THE 1940 WORLD SERIES WERE THE CINCINNATI REDS, WHO WITH A 100–53 RECORD HAD WON THEIR SECOND STRAIGHT N.L. PENNANT BY A WHOPPING 12 GAMES OVER RUNNERS-UP BROOKLYN. THE STRENGTH OF THE REDS WAS THEIR PITCHING STAFF: HEADLINED BY A PAIR OF ACES, BUCKY WALTERS (22–10) AND PAUL DERRINGER (20–12), AND A RELIEVER JOE BEGGS (12–3, 7 SAVES). THE REDS' CAPABLE OFFENSE WAS LED BY FIRST BASEMAN FRANK McCORMICK (.309, 19, 127), CATCHER ERNIE LOMBARDI (.319), AND 3RD BASEMAN BILL WERBER (.277, 12, 48).

Frank McCormick

Ernie Lombardi

Bill Werber

THE TEAMS SPLIT THE FIRST TWO GAMES IN CINCINNATI; DETROIT'S BOBO NEWSOM WINNING THE OPENER 7-2, THE REDS' BUCKY WALTERS THE 2ND GAME 5-3.

AFTER NEWSOM SHUT OUT THE REDS 8-0 IN GAME 5, THE TIGERS TOOK A 3-2 LEAD AND WERE POISED TO WIN THE FRANCHISE'S 2ND WORLD CHAMPIONSHIP. [15]

BACK IN CINCINNATI THE REDS EVENED THINGS AGAIN BEHIND WALTERS' 4-0 WHITEWASH-ING. FRED MADE HIS 1ST AND ONLY SERIES APPEARANCE IN THE GAME. [16]

THE REDS TOOK THE SERIES THE NEXT DAY, 2-1. THE LOSS MIGHT HAVE STUNG A LITTLE LESS HAD FRED KNOWN HE WOULD ONE DAY RETURN TO THE WORLD SERIES WITH ANOTHER CINCINNATI REDS TEAM.

FRED STARTED 1941 IN BUFFALO AND WOUND UP SPENDING THE ENTIRE SEASON WITH THE BISONS. HE TURNED IN ANOTHER SPECTACULAR YEAR. [17]

THERE WAS NOTHING LEFT FOR HIM TO PROVE IN THE MINOR LEAGUES; BUT LOOMING WAR CLOUDS DARK-ENED ANY THOUGHTS ABOUT HIS RETURN TO THE TIGERS IN 1942.

THE WORLD HAD EFFECTIVELY
BEEN AT WAR SINCE SEPTEMBER
1939 WHEN THE GERMANS
INVADED POLAND. THE U.S. WAS
TRYING TO REMAIN NEUTRAL,
BUT MOST PEOPLE FEARED THE
COUNTRY WOULD EVENTUALLY BE
DRAWN INTO THE CONFLICT.

ON SUNDAY DECEMBER 7, 1941, THE
JAPANESE ATTACKED PEARL HARBOR,
OFFICIALLY DRAGGING THE U.S. INTO
WORLD WAR II. AMERICA DECLARED
WAR ON JAPAN THE NEXT DAY AND ON
GERMANY AND ITALY 3 DAYS LATER. LIKE
HUNDREDS OF OTHER PROFESSIONAL
BALLPLAYERS, FRED RESPONDED TO THE
CALL OF DUTY. HE ENLISTED IN THE NAVY
AND WAS INDUCTED IN LATE OCTOBER.

FRED BECAME PART OF FORMER BOXING CHAMPION GENE TUNNEY'S PHYSICAL TRAINING PROGRAM AT THE NORFOLK (VA) NAVAL TRAINING STATION, WHERE HE SPENT MOST OF 1942 AND 1943.

BECAUSE OF HIS EXPERIENCE AS A HUNTER, FRED ALSO SERVED AS A SHOOTING RANGE INSTRUCTOR, BUT HIS MAIN OCCUPATION WAS TO PITCH FOR NAVY BALL TEAMS.

HE PLAYED IN SEVERAL SERVICE ALL-STAR GAMES AND WORLD SERIES AND WON 23 GAMES IN 1943.[18]

IN 1943 FRED MARRIED FORMER FRANKLIN HIGH CLASSMATE PATSY FINLEY. THEY WERE LATER BLESSED WITH FOUR CHILDREN: FRED JR. (BORN 1944), JOHN (1945), PATTY (1948), AND JOSEPH (1953).[19]

LONG PERIODS OF INACTION AND BOREDOM ALWAYS ACCOMPANY THE ANXIETY AND DANGER OF WAR, AND SOMETIME DURING WORLD WAR II FRED PICKED UP THE HABIT OF CIGARETTE SMOKING FROM HIS FELLOW SERVICEMEN.

IN 1944 FRED WAS TRANSFERRED TO HAWAII WHERE HE WAS STATIONED WHEN THE WAR ENDED IN 1945. HE WAS DISCHARGED ON OCTOBER 18, 1945.[20]

41

IN THE SPRING OF 1946 FRED JOINED A TIGERS BALLCLUB THAT WAS THE REIGNING CHAMPION OF BASEBALL, AS DETROIT HAD WON THE PREVIOUS FALL'S WORLD SERIES AGAINST THE CUBS.

HOPES WERE HIGH FOR A REPEAT BECAUSE OF THE TIGERS' VAUNTED PITCHING STAFF. A DETROIT SCRIBE REPORTED FROM SPRING TRAINING THAT THE CLUB "HAS AT LEAST SEVEN GOOD HURLERS." FRED WAS NOT EVEN MENTIONED IN THE STORY.[21]

VETERAN TIGERS CATCHER BIRDIE TEBBETS SAW THINGS DIFFERENTLY. HE WAS IMPRESSED WITH FRED'S CONTROL, MATURITY, AND CONFIDENCE AND PREDICTED A BIG YEAR FOR HIM.

AFTER 2 SCORELESS RELIEF APPEARANCES, FRED GOT HIS FIRST START ON MAY 18 AND SHUT OUT THE PHILADELPHIA A'S 2-0 ON 4 HITS, STRIKING OUT 9.

42

ON MAY 22 FRED RAN HIS SCORE-
LESS STREAK TO 18 INNINGS BEFORE
THE YANKEES KNOCKED HIM OUT OF
THE GAME IN THE 5TH INNING.

HE
REBOUNDED
WITH A 6-1
VICTORY
AGAINST
CLEVELAND
ON THE
29TH,
SOLIDIFYING
HIS PLACE
IN DETROIT'S
STARTING
ROTATION.

FRED JOINED
A VETERAN
STARTING
CREW
CONSISTING
OF DIZZY
TROUT, VIRGIL
TRUCKS,
AL BENTON,
AND
HAL
NEWHOUSER
ARGUABLY,
THE BEST
PITCHER IN
THE A.L.[22]

EVEN WITH THE LEAGUE'S BEST PITCHING
DETROIT HAD TROUBLE KEEPING PACE WITH
THE BOSTON RED SOX, WHO ALSO HAD GOOD
PITCHING PLUS A SUPERIOR DEFENSE LED BY
THEIR DP COMBO, JOHNNY PESKY AND BOBBY
DOERR.[23]

BOSTON BEAT FRED 11-6 ON JUNE
9, AND IN THAT GAME HE GAVE UP
THE LONGEST (502 FT.) HOME RUN
EVER HIT AT FENWAY PARK.[24]

THEY BEAT FRED AGAIN, 1-O AND 3-2, BUT FRED'S GUTSY STYLE OF PITCHING IMPRESSED THE SPORTSWRITERS, WHO BEGAN TO REFER TO HIM AS A "HARD LUCK" PITCHER.

FRED MADE HIS OWN LUCK ON JULY 17, SPINNING A 2-HIT SHUTOUT AGAINST THE YANKEES. ONLY PHIL RIZZUTO AND CHARLIE KELLER HIT SAFELY AGAINST HIM.

THE TIGERS' INABILITY TO BEAT THE RED SOX HEAD-TO-HEAD WAS THE DIFFERENCE, AND BOSTON COASTED TO THE PENNANT BY A 12-GAME MARGIN.

FRED HAD A LOT TO DO WITH DETROIT'S 2ND PLACE FINISH, AS HE WON HIS FINAL 6 STARTS, INCLUDING A VICTORY OVER THE GREAT BOB FELLER.[25]

NO ONE DOUBTED ANY LONGER THAT THE TIGERS' BIG INVESTMENT IN FRED HAD BEEN WORTH IT. IN THE FALL IT WAS REPORTED THAT DETROIT WAS OPEN TO TRADING ANY PLAYERS EXCEPT 6 UNTOUCHABLES, INCLUDING FREDDIE HUTCHINSON. TIGERS MANAGER STEVE O'NEILL EVEN PREDICTED THAT FRED WOULD WIN 20 GAMES IN 1947.[26]

RAINY WEATHER AND LACKADAISICAL TRAINING IN THE SPRING MADE THE TIGERS ILL-PREPARED FOR A RUN AT THE 1947 PENNANT. WORSE, THE OFF-SEASON TRADE OF AGING SLUGGER HANK GREENBERG TO THE PITTSBURGH PIRATES STUCK DETROIT'S OFFENSE IN NEUTRAL.

ONE OF THE TEAM'S FEW BRIGHT SPOTS WAS THE PITCHING OF FRED HUTCHINSON, WHOSE 6 CONSECUTIVE WINS IN APRIL AND MAY CATAPULTED HIM TO THE TOP OF THE A.L. PITCHING CHARTS.

FRED WAS ON HIS WAY TO A 20-WIN SEASON UNTIL HE HAD TO LEAVE THE GAME ON 5-19 AFTER 5 INNINGS BECAUSE OF A "LAME SHOULDER." HE PITCHED SPARINGLY FOR THE NEXT 2 MONTHS.

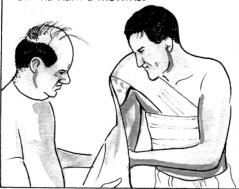

WHILE RECUPERATING FROM HIS INJURY, FRED GOT INTO A TUSSLE WITH N.Y. CATCHER RALPH HOUK IN THE MIDDLE OF A DONNYBROOK BETWEEN THE TIGERS AND THE VISITING YANKEES ON JUNE 5.[27]

TWO DAYS LATER FRED SPOKE REMORSE-FULLY ABOUT THE INCIDENT AT A HIGH SCHOOL BANQUET.[28]

FRED WAS BRILLIANT IN HIS RETURN TO THE STARTING ROTATION ON 7-18. HE STOPPED THE YANKEES COLD ON 2 HITS, ABRUPTLY ENDING THEIR 19-GAME WINNING STREAK.[29]

FRED ALSO CONTINUED TO HIT AS WELL (.302) AS A POSITION PLAYER, AND HE WAS OFTEN CALLED ON TO PINCH HIT. IN A DOUBLE-HEADER AT ST. LOUIS (8-13) HE CRACKED 3 HITS IN THE 1ST GAME AND A PH HOMER IN THE 2ND.

ANOTHER 2ND-PLACE FINISH BY THE TIGERS WAS HARDLY FRED'S FAULT. HE WON HIS FINAL 5 STARTS AND FINISHED WITH A TEAM-BEST 18-10 RECORD.[30]

18TH WIN
9-28-47   1-0
VS CLEVELAND

CLINCHED
2ND PLACE

FRED'S REWARD WAS A PAY RAISE FOR 1948 AND A PROMOTION TO THE FRONT OF THE ROTATION. MANAGER O'NEILL NOW CONSIDERED HUTCH AND HAL NEWHOUSER HIS ACES AND PLANNED TO BACK THEM UP WITH THE VETER- ANS DIZZY TROUT AND VIRGIL TRUCKS AND SOPHO- MORE ART HOUTTEMAN, WHO'D WON 7 GAMES IN HIS ROOKIE SEASON.[31]

FRED'S 1ST START IN THE TIGERS HOME OPENER WAS A DISASTER. HE LOST 8-2 AND GAVE UP 4 HOME RUNS, INCLUDING ONE TO THE A.L.'S 1ST BLACK PLAYER, LARRY DOBY.

THE LONG BALL WOULD PLAGUE FRED ALL SEASON. IN FACT, HE WOULD SET A NEW A.L. RECORD FOR HOME RUNS ALLOWED WITH 32.

AT THE END OF MAY THE YANKEES KNOCKED FRED OUT OF A GAME EARLY. HE LEFT WITH A 3-3 RECORD AND A RECURRENCE OF HIS SHOULDER INJURY. "THIS HAS ME PLENTY WORRIED," HE SAID.[32]

INDICATIVE OF THE RESPECT PLAYERS AROUND THE LEAGUE HAD FOR HIM, FRED WAS CHOSEN TO BE THE A.L. PLAYER REPRESENTATIVE. HE BEGAN STUDYING BASEBALL LAW AND THE PENSION PLAN.[33]

FRED REJOINED THE STARTING ROTATION ON JULY 1 AND PITCHED WELL IN A 9-5 DETROIT WIN. "MY SHOULDER DIDN'T BOTHER ME A BIT. I'M GOING TO START WINNING MORE GAMES FOR YOU," HE HAPPILY TOLD O'NEILL.

AS THE TIGERS AND FRED BOTH STRUGGLED TO STAY ABOVE .500, THE BIGGEST NEWS OF THE SUMMER BROKE: THE DEATH OF BABE RUTH, WHO DIED OF THROAT CANCER ON AUGUST 16.

MORE THAN 100,000 FANS PASSED BY THE BABE'S BIER IN THE ROTUNDA OF YANKEE STADIUM. A SOLEMN REQUIEM MASS, PRESIDED OVER BY FRANCIS CARDINAL SPELLMAN, WAS SAID FOR HIM ON AUGUST 19 AT NEW YORK'S ST. PATRICK'S CATHEDRAL.

WHEN AN INJURY ON AUGUST 29 KNOCKED THEIR BEST HITTER, GEORGE KELL, OUT FOR THE SEASON, THE WEAK-HITTING TIGERS WERE PRETTY MUCH FINISHED.

DETROIT TRUDGED HOME IN FIFTH PLACE, AND FRED ENDED UP WITH A 13–11 RECORD.(34)

THE TIGERS WANTED A TOUGHER MANAGER FOR 1949 AND GOT ONE: FORMER DETROIT FARM DIRECTOR RED ROLFE, WHO'D PLAYED 3RD BASE FOR FIVE N.Y. YANKEES WORLD CHAMPIONSHIP TEAMS.

FRED WANTED ANOTHER PAY RAISE BUT DIDN'T GET IT. AT LEAST HE DIDN'T TAKE A CUT.㉟

AS USUAL, HE GOT OFF TO A SLOW START. HE TOOK LOSING HARD, AND SOMETIMES HIS TEMPER GOT THE BEST OF HIM.㊱

THE NEW SKIPPER GOT MIXED RESULTS FROM OTHER "ROLFEMEN," AS THE TIGERS SANK INTO THE SECOND DIVISION. INJURED IN A BAD CAR WRECK, PITCHER ART HOUTTEMAN BEGAN THE SEASON ON THE DL, AND FORMER BONUS BABY DICK WAKEFIELD REMAINED INCONSISTENT AT BAT. ON THE OTHER HAND, CENTERFIELDER JOHNNY GROTH PLAYED HIMSELF INTO CONTENTION FOR THE A.L. ROOKIE OF THE YEAR AWARD, WHILE OUTFIELDER VIC WERTZ BECAME ONE OF THE TEAM'S TOP RBI PRODUCERS.

AFTER GIVING UP 3 HOME RUNS IN A 4-0 LOSS TO CHICAGO ON JULY 1, FRED WAS DEMOTED TO THE BULLPEN.

MANAGER ROLFE THOUGHT FRED NEEDED A NEW PITCH AND ASKED HIM TO WORK WITH COACH TED LYONS, A FORMER WHITE SOX ACE.

LYONS TAUGHT HUTCH THE KNUCKLE-BALL, WHICH FRED BEGAN USING IN HIS NEXT 7 APPEARANCES, ALL IN RELIEF.

ON JULY 6 FRED AND N.L. PLAYER REP DIXIE WALKER PRESENTED 5 IMPORTANT PROPOSITIONS TO THE M.L. EXECUTIVE COUNCIL, ALL OF WHICH WERE EVENTU-ALLY ADOPTED.[37]

THE SPORTING NEWS DUBBED FRED "THE COMEBACK KID" AFTER HIS BACK-TO-BACK SHUT OUTS OF WASHINGTON (7-27) AND PHILADELPHIA (7-31) SET HIM OFF ON AN 8-GAME WINNING STREAK.

FRED POSTED A CAREER-BEST ERA (2.96) AND WINNING PERCENTAGE (.682, 15-7), AND HIS TURNAROUND HELPED DETROIT RALLY TO A 4TH PLACE FINISH.[38]

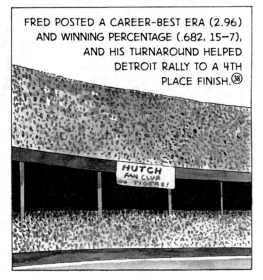

50

IN THE SPRING OF 1950 THE NORMALLY
SLOW-STARTING HUTCH, FOR ONCE, WAS
THE HOTTEST PITCHER IN CAMP. HE GAVE
UP ONLY ONE RUN ALL SPRING; AND WITH
HAL NEWHOUSER ON THE SHELF WITH A
SORE SHOULDER, FRED RECEIVED THE
FIRST OPENING DAY STARTING ASSIGNMENT
OF HIS MAJOR LEAGUE CAREER. HE
HELPED THE TIGERS GET OFF ON THE
RIGHT FOOT, GOING 7 INNINGS IN THEIR
7–6 WIN AT CLEVELAND.

VETERAN 2ND BASEMAN JERRY PRIDDY, OBTAINED FROM THE ST. LOUIS BROWNS, TEAMED WITH YOUNG SS JOHNNY LIPON TO STRENGTHEN THE TIGERS INFIELD, ...

...WHILE HOOT EVERS COMBINED WITH JOHNNY GROTH AND VIC WERTZ TO FORM ONE OF THE BEST OUTFIELD TRIOS IN BASEBALL. THE TIGERS WON 5 OF THEIR 1ST 6 AND JUMPED TO THE HEAD OF THE PACK.

EVER THE FEARLESS COMPETITOR, FRED CONTINUED TO RELY ON GUTS AND GUILE. IN A TYPICAL HUTCHINSON OUTING, HE GAVE UP 15 HITS DURING A COMPLETE GAME 16-5 WIN OVER THE A'S ON JUNE 2.

FRED ALSO REMAINED DANGEROUS AT BAT. IN ONE 2-GAME STRETCH HE WENT 7-10 WITH 6 RBI.

ON AUGUST 30 FRED LOST A 3-2 HEART-BREAKER TO WASHINGTON, A DEFEAT WHICH KNOCKED THE TIGERS OUT OF 1ST PLACE AFTER 81 DAYS.

THE FOLLOWING DAY HE WAS THROWN OUT OF THE GAME FOR ARGUING BALLS AND STRIKES WHILE SS LIPON BATTED.[39]

THREE WEEKS LATER FRED'S CLUTCH PITCHING BOOSTED DETROIT INTO A TIE FOR 1ST PLACE WITH THE YANKEES. (40)

UNFORTUNATELY, THE TIGERS DROPPED THEIR NEXT 3 GAMES TO THE INDIANS, FUMBLING ANY CHANCE OF COPPING THE PENNANT.

DETROIT'S OUTSTANDING FINAL RECORD (95–59) WAS ONLY GOOD ENOUGH FOR SECOND PLACE, 3 GAMES BEHIND THE CHAMPION NEW YORK PINSTRIPERS.

FRED'S 17 VICTORIES AGAIN MADE HIM ONE OF DETROIT'S BIGGEST WINNERS WITH ART HOUTTEMAN (18) AND HAL NEWHOUSER (16).

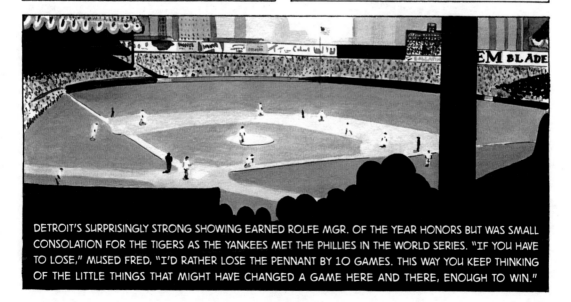

DETROIT'S SURPRISINGLY STRONG SHOWING EARNED ROLFE MGR. OF THE YEAR HONORS BUT WAS SMALL CONSOLATION FOR THE TIGERS AS THE YANKEES MET THE PHILLIES IN THE WORLD SERIES. "IF YOU HAVE TO LOSE," MUSED FRED, "I'D RATHER LOSE THE PENNANT BY 10 GAMES. THIS WAY YOU KEEP THINKING OF THE LITTLE THINGS THAT MIGHT HAVE CHANGED A GAME HERE AND THERE, ENOUGH TO WIN."

UNCLE SAM CAST A PALL OVER TIGERS HOPES FOR 1951 WHEN THE ARMY DRAFTED ACE ART HOUTTEMAN BEFORE THE SEASON STARTED.

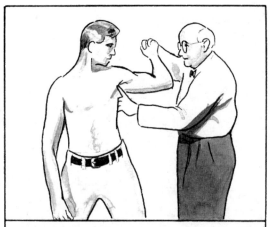

HAL NEWHOUSER'S AND DIZZY TROUT'S ON-GOING SORE ARM MISERIES ADDED TO DETROIT'S WOES.

WORST OF ALL, MOST OF THE LINEUP WENT INTO A SEASON LONG BATTING SLUMP. BY THE TIME THE ALL-STAR GAME AT BRIGGS STADIUM ROLLED AROUND (JULY 10), THE TIGERS STOOD AT 34–38, 12 GAMES BACK.

HUTCH HAD A 7–3 RECORD AT THE BREAK AND WAS NAMED TO THE A.L. ALL-STAR SQUAD BY MANAGER CASEY STENGEL.

HE PITCHED 3 INNINGS IN THE A.L.'S 8–3 LOSS, GIVING UP 3 RUNS, 2 ON A HR BY GIL HODGES.

THE FRUSTRATION OF THE TIGERS' POOR SEASON CAME TO A HEAD FOR FRED ON 8–14 IN A 6–5 LOSS AT CLEVELAND. HE WAS EJECTED FROM THE GAME AND HAD TO BE RESTRAINED FROM ACCOSTING THE UMPIRE.[41]

DETROIT'S DISAPPOINTING FINAL RECORD WAS THE TIGERS' WORST SINCE 1942.[42]

THE POOR SHOWING RESULTED IN THE FIRING OF G.M. BILLY EVANS, WHO WAS REPLACED BY FORMER TIGER GREAT CHARLIE GEHRINGER.

THE TIGERS LOST THEIR 1ST 8 GAMES OF 1952 AND LOOKED TERRIBLE DOING SO.[43]

THE NEWS-PAPERS REPORT-ED THAT THE PLAYERS WERE READY TO MUTINY AGAINST MANAGER ROLFE.[44]

THAT RUMOR WAS PROVED TO BE FALSE AFTER THE PLAYERS HELD A CLOSED DOOR MEETING...

Players ONLY!

...AND ISSUED A STATEMENT OF SUPPORT FOR ROLFE WHICH WAS READ BY HUTCH, THEIR PLAYER REPRESENTATIVE.[45]

NEVERTHELESS, THE SEASON CONTINUED TO BE A COMPLETE DISASTER, ...

...AND AFTER THE TIGERS LOST A JULY 4 DOUBLE-HEADER TO CLEVELAND THEY REMAINED MIRED IN LAST PLACE WITH A 23–47 RECORD.

ALL PRICES REDUCED

½ OFF!

TIGERS

THE NEXT DAY OWNER SPIKE BRIGGS HELD A PRESS CONFERENCE TO
ANNOUNCE SOME CHANGES: MANAGER RED ROLFE AND COACH DICK
BARTELL WERE BEING FIRED HE SAID. HE THANKED BOTH MEN FOR THEIR
SERVICE TO THE BALLCLUB AND WISHED THEM WELL. HE PAUSED FOR A
MOMENT, THEN SAID, "THE NEW MANAGER IS FRED HUTCHINSON."[46]

"He was the first manager I ever knew who believed in night school."

—St. Louis Cardinals General Manager Frank "The Trader" Lane

"He's a great guy to play for. If you can't play for him, you can't play for anybody."

Cardinals pitcher Jim Davis on Hutch after being traded from St. Louis to New York.

TECHNICALLY, FRED WAS NAMED MANAGER OF THE TIGERS ON AN INTERIM BASIS HAVING BEEN OFFERED THE JOB ONLY AFTER COACH TED LYONS TURNED IT DOWN. STILL ONLY 32 YEARS OLD, FRED IMMEDIATELY ANNOUNCED HE WOULD NOT PITCH ANYMORE SO HE COULD CONCENTRATE ON MANAGING. HE HAD PITCHED (MOSTLY IN RELIEF) IN ONLY 12 GAMES ALL SEASON ANYWAY, COMPILING A 2-1 RECORD IN 37 INNINGS.[1]

FRED HUTCHINSON

SOME SPORTSWRITERS WERE SKEPTICAL ABOUT FRED'S CHANCES, OPINING THAT PITCHERS SELDOM MAKE GOOD MANAGERS.②

NOT SO THE DETROIT PLAYERS, WHO CHEERED UPROARIOUSLY WHEN TOLD THE NEWS.

TIGERS FANS TOO WELCOMED HUTCH'S HIRING. THEY GAVE HIM A STANDING OVATION BEFORE HIS DEBUT ON JULY 5 AGAINST THE ST. LOUIS BROWNS, AND THE TEAM CAME THROUGH FOR THEIR NEW BOSS WITH A 5–0 WIN. THE TIGERS WON THE NEXT DAY TOO, BUT IT WAS A COSTLY VICTORY.

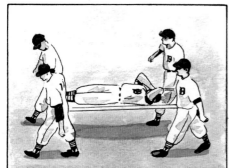

SECOND BASEMAN JERRY PRIDDY BROKE HIS ANKLE SLIDING INTO HOME AND WAS LOST FOR THE SEASON.

AFTER THE ALL-STAR BREAK, THE TEAM REVERTED TO FORM AND LOST 5 STRAIGHT.

IN AN UNUSUAL MOVE, HUTCH LEFT THE DUGOUT AND TOOK OVER THE 3RD BASE COACH-ING DUTIES HIMSELF. "I FEEL I CAN LEARN MORE OUT THERE," HE SAID.

IN ANOTHER SIGN OF HIS COMMIT-MENT, HE TOOK HIS NAME OFF THE ACTIVE PLAYER LIST ON JULY 22, ...③

...AND BOUGHT A HOUSE IN DETROIT FOR HIMSELF, PATSY, AND THE KIDS.

AS MUCH AS THE PLAYERS RESPECTED HUTCH, THEY WONDERED IF MANAGING WOULD CHANGE HIM.

WOULD HUTCH ENFORCE A CURFEW? WOULD HE STILL LET THEM PLAY CARDS IN THE CLUBHOUSE?

HUTCH TOLD THE PLAYERS TO HOLD A MEETING TO COME UP WITH SOME GUIDELINES FOR BEHAVIOR.

THE PLAYERS SET DOWN A CODE OF CONDUCT THAT HUTCH FOUND ACCEPTABLE.

"O.K. THESE ARE THE RULES," HE SAID. "ANYONE WHO BREAKS THEM WILL HAVE TO ANSWER TO ME."

YEARS LATER PITCHER TED GRAY REMEMBERED: "NOBODY BROKE THE RULES. WE WERE ALWAYS AFRAID OF HUTCH."

ONE OF THE FEW HIGHLIGHTS OF THE DISMAL SEASON CAME ON JULY 15 WHEN 1ST BASEMAN WALT DROPO TIED A M.L. RECORD BY GETTING HIS 12TH CONSECUTIVE HIT. DROPO HAD COME TO DETROIT IN A JUNE TRADE WITH BOSTON, ALONG WITH SS JOHNNY PESKY, 3RD BASEMAN FRED HATFIELD, OUTFIELDER DON LENHARDT, AND PITCHER BILL WIGHT. GEORGE KELL, DIZZY TROUT, HOOT EVERS, AND JOHNNY LIPON WENT THE OTHER WAY.④

SATCHEL PAIGE'S 12 INNING 1-0 WHITEWASH OF DETROIT ON 8-6 ILLUSTRATED THE TIGERS' INABILITY TO WIN CLOSE GAMES.

TWO DAYS LATER HUTCH SUFFERED HIS FIRST EJECTION AS MANAGER. HE'D BE TOSSED A COUPLE OF MORE TIMES BEFORE THE SEASON ENDED.⑤

THE PLAYERS CELEBRATED HUTCH'S BIRTHDAY (AND A RAINOUT IN CLEVELAND) ON THE TRAIN RIDE BACK TO DETROIT.

THE TIGERS CONTINUED THEIR ROSTER REVAMP, COMPLETING AN 8-PLAYER DEAL WITH ST. LOUIS ON AUGUST 14. KEY PLAYERS IN THE TRADE WERE BROWNS PITCHER NED GARVER AND THE TIGERS VIC WERTZ. TRYING TO CONSOLE THE YOUNG SLUGGER, HUTCH SAID, "WE HATE TO SEE YOU GO, VIC, BUT THE TEAM ISN'T WINNING, AND WE HAVE TO KEEP TRYING TO GET IT OUT OF THIS RUT. GOOD LUCK IN ST. LOUIS." ⑥

ON AUGUST 25 VIRGIL TRUCKS NO HIT THE YANKEES IN N.Y. AMAZINGLY, IT WAS HIS SECOND NO HITTER OF 1952 BUT ONLY HIS 5TH WIN OF THE SEASON.

WITH THE SEASON LOST DETROIT BEGAN CALLING UP PROMISING YOUNG PLAYERS FROM THE MINOR LEAGUES.

HUTCH ESPECIALLY LIKED A SWEET-SWINGING SS FRESH OUT OF THE UNIVERSITY OF WISCONSIN, HARVEY KUENN, WHO WENT 2-5 IN HIS M.L. DEBUT ON 9-6. ⑦

THE BOSTON PRESS CRITICIZED HUTCH FOR PLAYING YOUNGSTERS AGAINST THE RED SOX'S RIVALS.

"WE DIDN'T BRING THEM UP TO SIT ON THE BENCH," HE SAID. "ANYWAY, I DON'T SEE WHY WE SHOULD WORRY ABOUT THE PENNANT RACE. WE HAVE OUR OWN PROBLEMS."

DESPITE THE TEAM'S RECORD, EVERYONE FELT HUTCH WAS DOING A GOOD JOB, AND ON 9-13 HE SIGNED UP TO MANAGE DETROIT IN 1953.[8]

THE LAST HIGHLIGHT OF THE SEASON CAME ON 9-25 WHEN PRINCE HAL NEWHOUSER WON HIS 200TH M.L. GAME.[9]

THE TIGERS' DISTINCTION OF BEING THE ONLY A.L. TEAM TO NEVER LOSE 100 GAMES WAS OVER.

AMERICAN LEAGUE		
YANKEES	95	59
INDIANS	93	61
WHITE SOX	81	73
ATHLETICS	79	75
SENATORS	78	76
RED SOX	76	78
BROWNS	64	90
TIGERS	50	104

"I REMEMBER SOME SEASONS THAT I WAS SORRY TO SEE COME TO AN END," HUTCH SAID. "I'M GLAD THIS ONE IS OVER."[10]

67

THE FLURRY OF TRADING DONE IN 1952 HAD MADE DETROIT A YOUNGER TEAM, AND HUTCH
RAN SPRING TRAINING IN '53 LIKE A BASEBALL ACADEMY. DURING SKULL SESSIONS AT NIGHT
HE AND THE COACHES DRILLED THE PLAYERS ON RULES, SIGNALS, SITUATIONS, DEFENSIVE
COVERAGE, DEPORTMENT, AND PHILOSOPHY. URGING HIS CHARGES TO PLAY CONFIDENTLY,
HUTCH SAID, "DO SOME THINKING FOR YOURSELF, AND USE YOUR BEST JUDGMENT."[11]

HUTCH ALSO HAD SOME INTERESTING
ADVICE ABOUT DEALING WITH UMPIRES.

"DON'T SOUND OFF," HE SAID. "YOU
COULD BE WRONG. CLOSE PLAYS CAN
GO EITHER WAY."

THE TIGERS LOST THE OPENER TO BILL VEECK'S BROWNS 10-0 AND STARTED THE SEASON 2-7.⑫

HUTCH WAS NOT DISCOURAGED THOUGH. "WHEN OUR PITCHING IS RIGHT, WE ARE TOUGH," HE SAID.

ON MAY 3 ART HOUTTEMAN BLEW A WIN AGAINST THE YANKEES. THE NEXT DAY HE GOT THE WIN, STRIKING OUT MICKEY MANTLE TO END THE GAME.

"THANKS FOR GIVING ME ANOTHER CHANCE," HE SAID TO HUTCH. "YOU WENT OUT ON THE LIMB FOR ME."

A 10-31 RECORD AND 13 STRAIGHT LOSSES CAUSED RUMORS OF HUTCH'S IMPENDING DEPARTURE, ...⑬

...WHICH WERE DISMISSED BY OWNER SPIKE BRIGGS WHO SAID, "THAT'S A LOT OF BUNK. WE ARE GOING DOWN THE LINE WITH HUTCH."

A TRADE ON JUNE 15 PAID BIG DIVIDENDS. EX-INDIAN RAY BOONE CURED DETROIT'S HOT CORNER WOES AND TORE THE COVER OFF THE BALL.[14]

RAY BOONE
STARRING CLEVELAND INDIANS

DETROIT ALSO DEBUTED AN 18-YEAR-OLD BONUS BABY, AL KALINE, WHO WOULD BECOME ONE OF THE GREATEST PLAYERS IN TEAM HISTORY. KALINE GOT HIS FIRST HIT ON A GROUNDER THROUGH THE INFIELD ON 7-9. HE WOULD FINISH 1953 BATTING .250 AND END HIS 22-YEAR CAREER WITH 3,007 HITS, HAVING NEVER PLAYED A SINGLE MINOR LEAGUE GAME.[15]

LED BY KUENN AND BOONE THE TIGERS LEFT THE CELLAR BEHIND WITH A WIN OVER N.Y. ON 6-24.[16]

TO HELP HIS BELEAGUERED PITCHING STAFF, HUTCH ACTIVATED HIMSELF IN AUGUST AND MADE THE FINAL THREE APPEARANCES OF HIS CAREER.[17]

CONTINUING THEIR IMPROVED PLAY, DETROIT TIED THE M.L. RECORD ON 9-10 WITH THEIR 9TH STRAIGHT ERRORLESS GAME.[18]

The Sporting News

1953 FINAL STANDINGS
1ST NEW YORK YANKEES
2ND CLEVELAND INDIANS
3RD CHICAGO WHITE SOX
4TH BOSTON RED SOX
5TH WASHINGTON SENATORS
6TH DETROIT TIGERS
7TH PHILADELPHIA ATHLETICS
8TH ST LOUIS BROWNS

DETROIT'S ENDING IN 6TH PLACE FULFILLED HUTCH'S PROMISE THAT THE TEAM WOULD NOT FINISH IN THE BASEMENT AGAIN.[19]

HARVEY KUENN ALSO JUSTIFIED HUTCH'S FAITH IN HIM. HE BATTED .308, LED THE A.L. IN HITS (208), AND WAS NAMED ROOKIE OF THE YEAR.

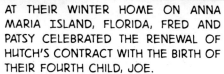

Baby's First Christmas 1953

AT THEIR WINTER HOME ON ANNA MARIA ISLAND, FLORIDA, FRED AND PATSY CELEBRATED THE RENEWAL OF HUTCH'S CONTRACT WITH THE BIRTH OF THEIR FOURTH CHILD, JOE.

HUTCH PROVED HE WAS STILL A GOOD ATHLETE BY WINNING A CELEBRITY GOLF TOURNAMENT IN JANUARY, ...[20]

...AND AT 35 HE WAS STILL THE YOUNGEST MANAGER IN THE M.L., AS HE BEGAN HIS SECOND FULL YEAR AT THE TIGERS HELM.

WHEN THE YANKEES PLUNKED DETROIT'S BEST HITTER IN A SPRING EXHIBITION GAME, HUTCH WARNED AGAINST IT HAPPENING IN THE REGULAR SEASON.

"WE'LL RETALIATE BY PITCHING AT THEIR HITTERS," HE SAID. "THAT MEANS YOGI BERRA AND ALL THE REST." [21]

BY THE TIME THE '54 SEASON OPENED, HUTCH HAD DECIDED TO IMPLEMENT A YOUTH MOVEMENT. FRANK BOLLING (2B), FRANK HOUSE (C), BILL TUTTLE (OF), AND AL KALINE (OF) PLAYED OFTEN AND WELL AND BECAME KNOWN AS "THE FOUR FRESHMEN."

STEVE GROMEK, NED GARVER, AND GEORGE ZUVERINK EMERGED AS HUTCH'S MOST RELIABLE STARTING PITCHERS. [22]

AS THE DAYS OF SPRING AND SUMMER HEATED UP, DETROIT'S HITTERS
COOLED OFF, WASTING MUCH SOLID PITCHING BY THE BIG THREE. AFTER
104 DAYS IN THE FIRST DIVISION, THE TIGERS WERE KNOCKED OUT OF 4TH
PLACE ON 7-24. THEY FINISHED IN 5TH, ONE GAME OUT OF 4TH, WITH A
68-86 RECORD. THE 8-GAME IMPROVEMENT OVER '53 PROVED THAT
HUTCH HAD THE TEAM MOVING IN THE RIGHT DIRECTION.[23]

WHILE WILLIE MAYS AND THE N.Y. GIANTS SWEPT CLEVELAND IN THE WORLD SERIES, ...

...HUTCH MET WITH THE DETROIT BRASS WHO RESISTED HIS DEMAND FOR A 2-YEAR CONTRACT.

"ONE YEAR IS ALL WE CAN DO," SAID OWNER BRIGGS FINALLY. "I'M TURN-ING IT DOWN," SAID HUTCH.

AND JUST LIKE THAT HUTCH'S 11-YEAR CAREER WITH THE DETROIT TIGERS WAS OVER.

TWO WEEKS LATER IT WAS ANNOUNCED THAT HUTCH WAS COMING HOME TO SEATTLE, TO MANAGE THE RAINIERS.[24]

OWNER EMIL SICK GAVE HUTCH A LIFETIME CONTRACT, WHICH ALSO ALLOWED HIM TO LEAVE FOR A MAJOR LEAGUE JOB AFTER ONE SEASON IN SEATTLE.[25]

74

THE P.C.L. IN 1955 WAS A HOT BED OF GOOD TEAMS LED BY SAVVY EXPERIENCED MANAGERS, SUCH AS SAN FRANCISCO'S LEFTY O'DOUL.㉖

THE HOLLYWOOD STARS, MANAGED BY BOBBY BRAGAN, WERE HEAVY FAVORITES TO WIN THE PENNANT.

HUTCH INHERITED AN OLD, 5TH-PLACE TEAM, SO HE CLEANED HOUSE AND BROUGHT 30 NEW PLAYERS TO SPRING TRAINING.㉗

HE HAD THE SCREEN IN FRONT OF SEATTLE'S DUGOUT REMOVED TO MAKE THE PLAYERS PAY CLOSE ATTENTION TO THE GAME.

AND HE ADOPTED A POLICY OF FINING PLAYERS FOR MENTAL MISTAKES, SUCH AS MISSING SIGNS.㉘

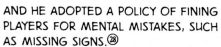

THE RAINIERS TOOK ON FRED'S PERSONALITY, AND THEIR SMART, AGGRESSIVE PLAY WON THEM PEPSI'S FIRST MONTHLY HUSTLE AWARD.㉙

75

SEATTLE'S STRONG PITCHING (BY ELMER SINGLETON, LOU KRETLOW, AND BILL KENNEDY) KEPT THE CLUB CLOSE TO THE TOP.

UNHAPPY ABOUT THE TEAM'S WEAK HITTING, HUTCH ORDERED EXTRA BATTING PRACTICE.

HE ALSO HAD HIS BATTERS FILMED SO THAT THEY MIGHT DETECT FLAWS IN THEIR SWINGS.

AS A SUGGESTIVE JOKE, G.M. DEWEY SORIANO GAVE HUTCH SOMETHING TO HELP HIM DEAL WITH HIS TEMPER.

GOING INTO JUNE THE RAINIERS WERE IN 3RD PLACE. INJURIES THREATENED TO KNOCK THEM OUT OF CONTENTION, BUT HUTCH ALWAYS FOUND CAPABLE REPLACEMENTS, SUCH AS EX—BIG LEAGUE PITCHERS LARRY JANSEN, RYNE DUREN, AND EWELL BLACKWELL AND SS VERN STEPHENS.

76

THE RAINIERS PLAYED 61 ONE-RUN GAMES AND LED THE LEAGUE IN COME-FROM-BEHIND WINS.

THIS EXCITING BASEBALL BROUGHT THE CROWDS BACK TO SICK'S STADIUM, AND ATTENDANCE DOUBLED OVER 1954.[30]

ON JULY 17 SEATTLE TOOK OVER FIRST PLACE AND STAYED THERE THE REST OF THE SEASON.

HUTCH'S BIRTHDAY WAS CELEBRATED ON AUGUST 12, AND AMONG HIS PRESENTS: A BRAND NEW STATION WAGON!

SEATTLE CLINCHED THE PENNANT ON THE NEXT TO THE LAST DAY OF THE SEASON, AND HUTCH EASILY WON THE LEAGUE'S MANAGER OF THE YEAR AWARD.

HE WAS UNIVERSALLY PRAISED FOR WINNING WITH A MEDIOCRE CLUB THAT HAD NO .300 HITTERS AND USED 8 DIFFERENT 2ND BASEMEN.[31]

FRED'S REWARD WAS NOT LONG IN COMING: HIS SECOND BIG LEAGUE MANAGING JOB, WITH THE STORIED ST. LOUIS CARDINALS.[32]

ON OCTOBER 12 HUTCH WAS GIVEN A 2-YEAR CONTRACT BY THE CARDS' NEW G.M., FRANK LANE.

YEARS BEFORE AS THE G.M. OF THE CHICAGO WHITE SOX, LANE HAD SEEN HUTCH CONDUCTING SKULL SESSIONS ONE EVENING FOR HIS DETROIT PLAYERS IN A HOTEL LOBBY. LANE HAD DECIDED THEN THAT IF HE WERE EVER IN A POSITION AGAIN OF NEEDING TO HIRE A FIELD MANAGER, HE'D OFFER THE JOB TO FRED IF HE WERE AVAILABLE. LANE AND FRED HAD THEIR WORK CUT OUT FOR THEM, AS THEY TOOK OVER A CLUB THAT HAD FINISHED IN 7TH PLACE IN 1955.

IN LATE NOVEMBER HUTCH MET WITH HIS COACHES IN ST. LOUIS TO DISCUSS PLANS FOR THE 1956 SEASON.(33)

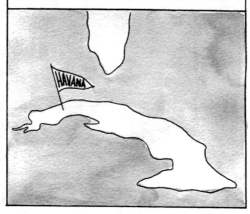

IN JANUARY HUTCH FLEW TO CUBA TO WATCH TOP PROSPECT VINEGAR BEND MIZELL PITCH WINTER LEAGUE BALL.(34)

SPRING TRAINING WENT WELL, WITH THE CARDS POSTING THE BEST EXHIBITION GAMES RECORD IN BASEBALL.(35)

LED BY YOUNGSTERS KEN BOYER (3B), WALLY MOON (1B-OF), AND DON BLAS-INGAME (2B), THE CARDS STAYED HOT, ...

...AND BEGAN REMINDING FANS OF THE SPIRIT OF PEPPER MARTIN AND THE OLD GAS HOUSE GANG.(36)

AT THE SAME TIME LANE'S INCESSANT TRADING KEPT THE ROSTER IN SUCH FLUX...(37)

...THAT AFTER RED SCHOENDIENST WAS SHIPPED TO THE GIANTS ON JUNE 14 ONLY 6 PLAYERS FROM THE 1955 SQUAD REMAINED.[38]

COMPETITIVE AS EVER, HUTCH GOT THE THUMB IN SEVERAL GAMES AND EVEN DREW A 3-GAME SUSPENSION ON 6-29 FOR DISPUTING A HR CALL TOO VOCIFEROUSLY.[39]

STILL, HUTCH RETAINED HIS SENSE OF HUMOR. AFTER A BAD HOP SINGLE OVER THE GLOVE OF BOYER NEARLY COST THE CARDS A WIN, HE TOSSED SOME OBJECTS OUT OF THE DUGOUT AS A COMMENT ON THE GROUNDSKEEPING AT EBBETS FIELD.[40]

IN THE END THE CARDS SIMPLY DID NOT HAVE THE POWER TO COMPETE WITH THE TOP CLUBS.

NEVERTHELESS, WHEN LINDY McDANIEL BEAT THE CUBS ON 9-25 ST. LOUIS CLINCHED 4TH PLACE, AN IMPROVEMENT OF 3 PLACES IN THE STANDINGS.[41]

IN MID-JANUARY '57 HUTCH FLEW TO WEST GERMANY TO HELP RUN BASEBALL CLINICS SPONSORED BY THE U.S.A.F.[42]

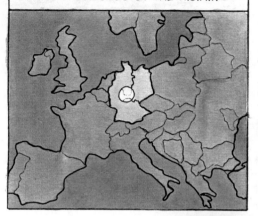

BEFORE HE LEFT HE SPOKE AT A TEAM BANQUET EMCEED BY BROADCASTER AND FORMER ST. LOUIS CATCHER JOE GARAGIOLA.

IT WAS GARAGIOLA WHO NICKNAMED HUTCH "THE BEAR" FOR HIS IMPOSING STRENGTH AND FEARSOME DEMEANOR.[43]

IN DEFENDING ALL THE MOVES THE CARDS HAD MADE, HUTCH SAID, "IF YOU'RE AFRAID TO GAMBLE IN BASE-BALL, YOU'D BETTER GET OUT."[44]

POOR FIELDING AND DISAPPOINTING STARTING PITCHING, ESPECIALLY BY MIZELL, CAUSED ANOTHER SLOW CARDINALS' START.[45]

HUTCH'S BULLPEN BECAME WORN OUT, AS HE USED 88 PITCHERS IN THE 1ST 29 GAMES OF 1957.

ON MAY 23 WITH THE CARDS IN 6TH PLACE, HUTCH MOVED KEN BOYER TO CF AND INSTALLED ROOKIE EDDIE KASKO AT 3B.

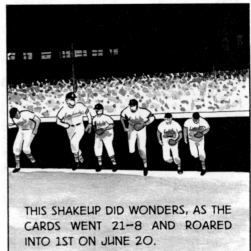

THIS SHAKEUP DID WONDERS, AS THE CARDS WENT 21-8 AND ROARED INTO 1ST ON JUNE 20.

LEADING THE WAY AS USUAL: STAN MUSIAL, WHO SET A N.L. RECORD BY PLAYING IN 823 STRAIGHT GAMES, ...[46]

...AND ROOKIE SENSATION VON McDANIEL WHO PITCHED 17 CONSECUTIVE SCORELESS INNINGS TO BEGIN HIS M.L. CAREER.

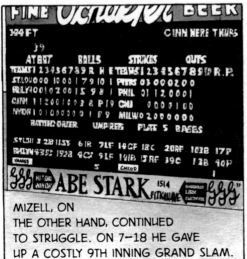

MIZELL, ON THE OTHER HAND, CONTINUED TO STRUGGLE. ON 7-18 HE GAVE UP A COSTLY 9TH INNING GRAND SLAM.

HUTCH WAS CRITICIZED FOR STICKING WITH MIZELL, BUT HIS COACHING AND SUPPORT HELPED TURN THE PITCHER AROUND.[47]

THROUGH JULY AND ON INTO AUGUST THE CARDS BATTLED WARREN SPAHN AND THE BRAVES FOR SUPREMACY.

THEN DISASTER: A 9-GAME LOSING STREAK, INCLUDING 6 LOSSES TO THE 7TH PLACE CUBS.[48]

N.Y. SPORTSWRITER DAN DANIEL REPORTED THAT HUTCH WAS ON THE "HOT SEAT," BUT FRED DIDN'T PANIC.

BEFORE THE NEXT GAME HE POSTED A FAKE LINEUP OF NAMES OF PLAYERS' KIDS, THE TRAINER, AND THE CLUBHOUSE MAN.

OFFICIAL BATTING ORDER	DATE
1 SMITTY	
2 FRANKIE	
3 DILLY BOYER	
4 IKE	
5 DICK NIXON	
6 PAT NIXON	
7 JOHNNY	
8 PETEY	
9 JULIA	
MGR SIGNATURE	

THE AMUSED AND RELAXED CARDINALS THEN REBOUNDED TO TAKE 3 OF 4 FROM THE HEAVY-HITTING BRAVES.

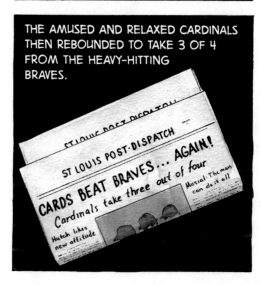

ST LOUIS POST-DISPATCH

CARDS BEAT BRAVES... AGAIN!

Cardinals take three out of four

Musial: The man can do it all

Hutch likes new attitude

WHEN HENRY AARON ACCUSED THE CARDINALS OF THROWING AT HIM, HUTCH SAID, "I DON'T TELL MY PITCHERS TO DELIBERATELY THROW AT ANY HITTER."[49]

WHILE IN YET ANOTHER FRACAS WITH THE UMPIRES, HUTCH WAS PUSHED BY BILL BAKER ON 8–31.[50]

HUTCH SAID LATER THAT HE HOPED THE LEAGUE WOULD NOT PUNISH BAKER.

TRY AS THEY MIGHT, THE CARDS COULD NOT CATCH THE BRAVES. AFTER MILWAUKEE BEAT ST. LOUIS ON 9–23 TO WIN THE PENNANT, HUTCH WAS AMONG THE 1ST TO CONGRATULATE HIS COUNTERPART, FRED HANEY. "YOU DESERVED TO WIN IT— YOU'VE GOT A GREAT CLUB," HE SAID.

WHEN THE CARDS BESTED THE BRAVES 2 DAYS LATER BEHIND LINDY McDANIEL, THEY CLINCHED SECOND PLACE.

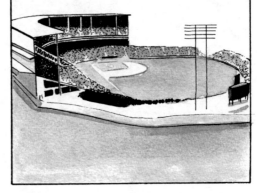

ABOUT HIS OWN PLAYERS HUTCH SAID, "THEY GAVE ME ALL THEY HAD AND I'M PROUD OF 'EM."

TO REWARD EIGHT OF HIS VETERANS, HUTCH LET THEM SKIP THE FINAL SERIES OF THE YEAR.[51]

AND EVEN THOUGH THE CARDS LOST ALL 3 GAMES TO CHICAGO, THEIR 87 WINS WAS THE MOST FOR ST. LOUIS SINCE 1952.

AMONG THE PLAYERS MOST RESPONSIBLE FOR THE CARDINALS' TURNAROUND: PITCHERS LINDY McDANIEL, LARRY JACKSON, AND SAM JONES AND THE GREAT STAN MUSIAL, WHO DESPITE INJURIES WON HIS 7TH N.L. BATTING TITLE (.351).

HUTCH SIGNED A NEW CONTRACT ON 9-28, AND HE WAS LATER NAMED N.L. MANAGER OF THE YEAR BY *THE SPORTING NEWS* AND U.P.I. HE WAS NOW WIDELY RECOGNIZED AS ONE OF THE BEST MANAGERS IN THE BIG LEAGUES.

85

CHAPTER 4

Building Towards a Winner, 1959–1960

"It's the pitcher's game for the first five innings. After that, it's mine."

Fred Hutchinson

IN NOVEMBER THE CARDS HIRED BING DEVINE TO REPLACE G.M. FRANK LANE WHO LEFT FOR CLEVELAND.

ON DECEMBER 11 THE CARDINALS TRADED FOR A PROMISING ROOKIE CENTERFIELDER, CURT FLOOD.

FLOOD WOULD HAVE A SOLID ROOKIE SEASON AND GO ON TO HELP LEAD ST. LOUIS TO 3 PENNANTS.

IN JANUARY HUTCH AND DEVINE WATCHED ST. LOUIS PROSPECTS PLAY IN THE DOMINICAN LEAGUE.

AFTER LOSING 4 OF THEIR 1ST 5 GAMES OF THE '58 SEASON TO THE CUBS, THE CARDINALS TOOK THEIR FIRST FLIGHT TO THE WEST COAST, FLYING FROM CHICAGO TO SAN FRANCISCO, THE NEW HOME OF THE FORMER N.Y. GIANTS.

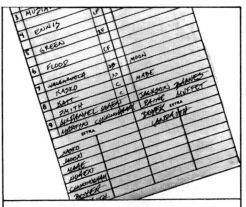

FIGHTING TO LIFT THE CARDS OUT OF LAST PLACE, HUTCH TIED A M.L. RECORD BY USING 24 MEN IN A 12-8 LOSS ON MAY 6.

FIVE DAYS LATER HE SET ANOTHER RECORD, USING 10 PINCH HITTERS IN A DOUBLE-HEADER.

ON MAY 13 HUTCH HELD STAN MUSIAL, SITTING ON 2,999 HITS, OUT OF THE STARTING LINEUP IN CHICAGO.①

MUSIAL WAS ABOUT TO BECOME THE FIRST BATTER TO REACH 3,000 HITS SINCE PAUL WANER IN 1942, ...

...AND HUTCH WANTED TO GIVE MUSIAL THE CHANCE TO RECORD THE HISTORIC HIT THE NEXT DAY IN ST. LOUIS.

HOWEVER, WHEN THE CARDS, LOSING 3-1, RALLIED IN THE SIXTH INNING, HUTCH SENT "THE MAN" UP TO PINCH HIT.

WITH ONE OUT, A RUNNER ON THIRD, AND A 2-2 COUNT, THE CUBS MOE DRABOWSKY THREW A CURVE...

...WHICH MUSIAL LINED INTO THE LF CORNER FOR AN RBI DOUBLE.

HUTCH CONGRATULATED MUSIAL ON THE FIELD, AND AFTER THE GAME TOLD HIM, "I'M SORRY. I KNOW YOU WANTED TO GET IT IN ST. LOUIS, BUT I NEEDED YOU."

ON MAY 20 THE CARDS SENT AL DARK TO CHICAGO FOR JIM BROSNAN. HUTCH HAD NOT FORGOTTEN HOW "BROZ" HAD BEATEN HIS SEATTLE CLUB 5 TIMES IN 1955. ALTHOUGH JIM WON HIS FIRST 3 STARTS, HUTCH LATER TURNED HIM INTO A RELIEVER.

THE CARDS SNEAKED INTO 2ND IN JUNE BUT WERE DONE IN BY A 9-20 MARK IN JULY.

AS A PRECAUTION THE FRUSTRATED HUTCH FOUND A WAY TO KEEP HIS HANDS AWAY FROM THE UMPIRES.

CREDITING HUTCH WITH HIS RESURGENCE, "SAD" SAM JONES PITCHED EXCELLENT BALL AND LED THE N.L. IN STRIKEOUTS,...②

...BUT TOO MANY OTHER CARDINALS HAD SUB-PAR SEASONS.③

ST. LOUIS WAS ELIMINATED FROM THE PENNANT RACE ON 9-12, AND HUTCH WAS FIRED THE NEXT DAY.④

FRED WATCHED THE NEXT 3 GAMES FROM THE PRESS BOX, THEN LEFT FOR SEATTLE TO VISIT HIS MOTHER.

ON OCTOBER 11 HUTCH RE-JOINED THE SEATTLE RAINIERS, THIS TIME AS MANAGER AND G.M. [5]

THE RAINIERS WERE NOW AFFILIATED WITH THE CINCINNATI REDS.

IN MARCH 1958 HUTCH SCOUTED THE CARDINALS' AND TIGERS' FLORIDA TRAINING CAMPS. IN LAKELAND HE TOOK PART IN A THREE-DAY CELEBRATION OF THE 25TH ANNIVERSARY OF DETROIT'S 1934 WORLD CHAMPIONSHIP TEAM. [6]

HUTCH HAD A VETERAN-LADEN CLUB, LED BY OUTFIELDER ELMER VALO, ...

...BUT INJURIES AND ANEMIC HITTING QUICKLY TURNED SEATTLE INTO THE DOORMAT OF THE P.C.L.

MEAN-WHILE, IN CINCINNATI THE REDS WERE STRUGGLING UNDER THE LEADERSHIP OF MAYO SMITH.

THE REDS WERE SCORING RUNS IN BUNCHES BUT COULDN'T GET ANYBODY OUT.

ON JULY 8 THE REDS FIRED SMITH AND HIRED HUTCH TO REPLACE HIM. (7)

SMITH LATER MANAGED THE DETROIT TEAM THAT WON THE 1968 WORLD SERIES.

ON JULY 17 HUTCH CALLED UP JAY HOOK, ONE OF HIS BEST PITCHERS AT SEATTLE. (8)

1ST MLB WIN
6-1-59
VS
CHI CUBS

THE NEXT DAY THE ROOKIE HOOK EARNED HIS FIRST M.L. VICTORY.

Brooks Lawrence

Bob Purkey

Jim O'Toole

Joe Nuxhall

TO FURTHER HELP THE PITCHING STAFF, HUTCH MOVED JIM BROSNAN TO THE BULLPEN AND ESTABLISHED A REGULAR ROTATION OF DON NEWCOMBE, BOB PURKEY, HOOK, JIM O'TOOLE, AND JOE NUXHALL.

Johnny Temple

Vada Pinson

Gus Bell

Frank Robinson

LED BY THEIR FIRST 4 BATTERS, THE REDS OFFENSE CONTINUED TO ROLL. LEADOFF MAN JOHNNY TEMPLE BATTED .311, WHILE 2ND YEAR CENTERFIELDER VADA PINSON (.316, 20, 84) BLOSSOMED INTO A STAR, SETTING CLUB RECORDS FOR RUNS (131) AND DOUBLES (47). RIGHT FIELDER GUS BELL HAD THE BEST RBI-YEAR (115) OF HIS CAREER AND WAS FOLLOWED BY FRANK ROBINSON (1B), WHO TURNED IN AN MVP-CALIBER PERFORMANCE (.311, 36, 125).

95

HUTCH HELPED ROOKIE PITCHER JIM O'TOOLE REDUCE HIS WILDNESS.

HE ALSO PREVAILED ON HAPPY-GO-LUCKY ED BAILEY TO TAKE THE GAME MORE SERIOUSLY, ...

...BUT A SEASON-ENDING INJURY TO SS ROY McMILLAN ON 8-11 SERIOUS-LY HURT THE DEFENSE. [9]

WORSE, THE TEAM LACKED A BONA FIDE CLOSER AND LOST NUMEROUS GAMES IN THE LATE INNINGS. [10]

UNDER HUTCH'S GUIDANCE THE REDS IMPROVED BY 14 GAMES, ...

...BUT THEIR OVERALL RECORD OF 74-80 LEFT THEM IN FIFTH PLACE, 13 GAMES BEHIND L.A.

ON DEC. 6 THE REDS BOLSTERED THEIR BULLPEN BY TRADING FOR RELIEVER BILL HENRY.

ON DEC. 15 THEY MADE AN EVEN BIGGER DEAL, ACQUIRING 19-GAME WINNER CAL MCLISH...

...AND VETERAN 2ND BASEMAN BILLY MARTIN FROM CLEVELAND.⑪

REDS FANS WERE NOT HAPPY BECAUSE THEY LOST POPULAR JOHNNY TEMPLE IN THE SWAP.⑫

LITTLE DID THEY KNOW THAT THROW-IN GORDY COLEMAN WOULD TURN OUT TO BE THE BEST PLAYER IN THE TRADE.

ON JAN. 23 HUTCH WAS HON-ORED AT A BANQUET ALONG WITH 97 YEAR OLD EX-REDLEG "DUMMY" HOY.

JIM BROSNAN'S DIARY OF THE 1959 SEASON HIT THE BOOKSTORES IN THE SPRING...⑬

PROMPTING HUTCH TO SAY: "I DON'T CARE WHAT BROZ WRITES OR SAYS AS LONG AS HE PITCHES WELL."

HOPES WERE HIGH IN CINCINNATI AS THE 1960 SEASON STARTED. HUTCH'S LINEUP ON OPENING DAY CONSISTED OF SIX RETURNING REGULARS (CATCHER ED BAILEY, 1ST BASEMAN FRANK ROBINSON, SS ROY McMILLAN, 3RD BASEMAN ED KASKO, AND OUTFIELDERS GUS BELL AND VADA PINSON) PLUS TWO NEWCOMERS: 2ND BASEMAN BILLY MARTIN AND YOUNG TONY GONZALEZ, WHO'D COME OUT OF NOWHERE IN SPRING TRAINING TO WIN THE 3RD OUTFIELD SPOT.⑭

HOME RUNS BY McMILLAN AND GONZALEZ HELPED THE REDS TAKE THE OPENER 9-4...[15]

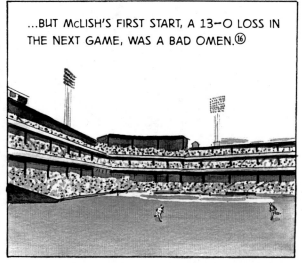

...BUT McLISH'S FIRST START, A 13-0 LOSS IN THE NEXT GAME, WAS A BAD OMEN.[16]

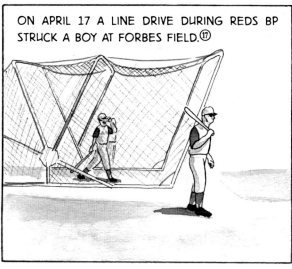

ON APRIL 17 A LINE DRIVE DURING REDS BP STRUCK A BOY AT FORBES FIELD.[17]

HUTCH PRESENTED THE LAD WITH A NEW BASEBALL, WHICH CHANGED HIS TEARS INTO A BIG SMILE.

AFTER LOSING TO THE PIRATES 13-2 ON MAY 1 THE 4-11 REDS DROPPED INTO LAST PLACE.[18]

THE NEXT DAY IN THE 8TH INNING OF THE REDS 6-5 WIN AT L.A. VADA PINSON GOT INTO A RUNDOWN.

HE RAN OVER PITCHER ROGER CRAIG, WHO BROKE HIS COLLAR BONE IN THE FALL.

THE FOLLOWING DAY 3 DIFFERENT DODGERS PITCHERS THREW AT PINSON.[19]

STAN WILLIAMS ALSO THREW A WILD PITCH OVER THE HEAD OF FRANK ROBINSON AND EXCHANGED ANGRY WORDS WITH HIM.

AFTER THE REDS' 5-3 WIN HUTCH SAID HE DIDN'T MIND THE PURPOSE PITCH TO ROBBY SINCE IT PLATED THE REDS AN INSURANCE RUN.

THE REDS STRETCHED THEIR WIN STREAK TO 9 WHEN JIM O'TOOLE SHUT OUT THE PHILLIES ON MAY 13.

TWO DAYS LATER RELIEVER RAUL SANCHEZ STIRRED THE POT AGAIN.

IN THE 8TH INNING WITH THE REDS TRAILING BADLY SANCHEZ HIT THREE PHILADELPHIA BATTERS.[20]

THIS INCENSED PHILLIES MANAGER GENE MAUCH WHO CHARGED THE MOUND.

A FULL-FLEDGED 12-MINUTE BRAWL ENSUED, DURING WHICH...

BILLY MARTIN EXCHANGED BLOWS WITH PITCHER GENE CONLEY, ...

...AND FUTURE HALL OF FAMERS FRANK ROBINSON AND ROBIN ROBERTS WENT AT IT.

BECAUSE OF THE HEROICS OF A FEW
PLAYERS, SUCH AS ED BAILEY (WHOSE 9TH
INNING GRAND SLAM BEAT THE BRAVES ON
MAY 27), BOB PURKEY (THE TEAM'S MOST
DEPENDABLE STARTER), AND JIM
BROSNAN (WHO WON GAMES ON MAY 27
AND MAY 30 WITH $7^2/_3$ INNINGS OF
SCORELESS RELIEF), THE REDS BUILT A
22–18 RECORD BY MAY 30. HOWEVER,
BECAUSE OF SLUMPS BY ROBINSON,
PINSON, AND BELL AND DISAPPOINTING
SEASONS BY PITCHERS McLISH AND DON
NEWCOMBE, THE TEAM SAGGED TO 26–
27 AFTER A 3–1 LOSS IN L.A. ON JUNE
21, NEVER ROSE ABOVE .500 AGAIN,
AND SETTLED INTO SIXTH PLACE.

WHEN THE REDS KICKED AWAY A GAME ON JUNE 3, HUTCH'S INFAMOUS TEMPER EXPLODED.[21]

THE BRAVES SCORED THREE 8TH-INNING RUNS WITH THE AID OF 2 BUNTS...[22]

...AND A THROWING ERROR TO WIN 4–1.[23]

THE BEAR BUSTED OUT EVERY LIGHT ON THE WAY TO THE CLUBHOUSE, ...

...FLIPPED OVER THE POST-GAME FOOD TABLE, ...

...AND RIPPED THE JERSEY RIGHT OFF HIS BODY.

ON JUNE 16 THE REDS RE-ACQUIRED WALLY POST, WHO WOULD BLAST 17 HOME RUNS IN 77 GAMES.[24]

ON JUNE 20 HUTCH STARTED DON NEWCOMBE IN AN EXHIBITION GAME...

...SO THAT "NEWK" COULD PROVE HE WAS REGAINING HIS 1959 FORM.

HOWEVER, BECAUSE HE WANTED TO LEAVE EARLY TO WATCH A BOXING MATCH NEWCOMBE PUT IN A HALF-HEARTED EFFORT.[25]

HUTCH DROPPED HIM FROM THE ROTATION, AND GABE PAUL LATER SOLD HIM TO CLEVELAND.

HUTCH WAS ALSO DISPLEASED WITH JIM O'TOOLE FOR GETTING MARRIED ON JULY 2.

THE NEXT DAY O'TOOLE GAVE UP 3 RUNS IN THE 1ST INNING ON RON SANTO'S FIRST M. L. HOME RUN.

THE CUBS KNOCKED O'TOOLE OUT IN THE 5TH AND WON THE GAME 7-5.

"I DIDN'T SCHEDULE O'TOOLE'S WEDDING," SAID HUTCH WHEN ASKED WHY HE DIDN'T GIVE JIM THE DAY OFF.

ON JULY 24 GORDY COLEMAN, UP FROM SEATTLE, HIT A HR IN HIS FIRST M. L. AT BAT.[26]

THE NEXT DAY SS LEO CARDENAS, 3B CLIFF COOK, AND P JIM MALONEY ARRIVED FROM THE MINORS.

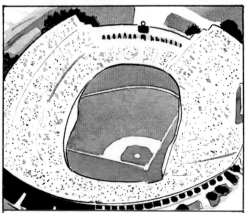

ON JULY 27 HUTCH ORDERED EXTRA BATTING PRACTICE AT THE L.A. COLISEUM.[27]

IT DID LITTLE GOOD AS DON DRYSDALE SHUT OUT THE REDS 2-0. [28]

MORE ENCOURAGING: THE DEBUT OF JIM MALONEY WHO GAVE UP ONE RUN IN 7 INNINGS.

THE POTENTIAL OF MALONEY, AGED 20, ALONG WITH THAT OF 23-YEAR-OLDS O'TOOLE AND WORKHORSE JAY HOOK, GAVE THE REDS HOPE FOR THE FUTURE. "OUR YOUNG PITCHERS ARE DOING GREAT," SAID HUTCH. "NOW, IF WE CAN JUST SCORE THEM SOME RUNS."

ON AUG. 2 THE REDS ACQUIRED ANOTHER RELIABLE ARM FOR THEIR BULLPEN, LEFTY MARSHALL BRIDGES.

ON AUG. 5 N.L. PRESIDENT WARREN GILES SUSPENDED BILLY MARTIN FOR 5 DAYS.

IT WAS TOO LITTLE TOO LATE, BUT ON AUG. 7 THE REDS EXPLODED FOR AN 18–4 WIN IN THE FIRST GAME OF A DOUBLE-HEADER IN ST. LOUIS. ROOKIE CLIFF COOK WENT 5–5. BATTING .208 FOR THE SEASON, HE WASN'T THE ANSWER TO THE CLUB'S PROBLEM AT 3RD BASE.

JIM MALONEY BEAT THE BRAVES 5–3 IN THE FIRST GAME OF A DOUBLE-HEADER ON AUG. 15 TO EARN HIS FIRST M.L. VICTORY.

THE GAME WAS MARRED BY YET ANOTHER MAJOR BRAWL.

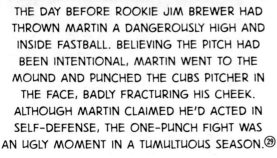

THE DAY BEFORE ROOKIE JIM BREWER HAD THROWN MARTIN A DANGEROUSLY HIGH AND INSIDE FASTBALL. BELIEVING THE PITCH HAD BEEN INTENTIONAL, MARTIN WENT TO THE MOUND AND PUNCHED THE CUBS PITCHER IN THE FACE, BADLY FRACTURING HIS CHEEK. ALTHOUGH MARTIN CLAIMED HE'D ACTED IN SELF-DEFENSE, THE ONE-PUNCH FIGHT WAS AN UGLY MOMENT IN A TUMULTUOUS SEASON.[29]

107

AS FRANK ROBINSON SLID AGGRESSIVE-LY INTO 3RD BASE IN THE 7TH INNING...

...HE AND EDDIE MATHEWS IMMEDI-ATELY BEGAN EXCHANGING PUNCHES.

ROBINSON GOT THE WORST OF IT AND LEFT THE GAME WITH A BLOODY NOSE, A CUT CHEEK, AND A BLACK EYE.

AMAZINGLY, FRANK NOT ONLY PLAYED IN THE NIGHTCAP, HE ALSO BEAT THE BRAVES ALMOST SINGLE-HANDEDLY.

HE REACHED BASE 4 TIMES, HIT A DOUBLE AND A HR, ...

...AND ROBBED MATHEWS OF A HIT WITH A DIVING CATCH INTO THE STANDS.[30]

AS FOR HUTCH, HE WAS MIFFED WHEN GILES FELT NO NEED TO DISCIPLINE MATHEWS, AS HE HAD MARTIN.

ON AUG. 30 ERNIE BANKS' NINTH INNING HR OFF JOE NUXHALL BEAT THE REDS 5-4.

HIS 1-7 RECORD HAD MADE HOME-TOWN BOY NUXHALL THE FAVORITE TAR-GET OF THE CROSLEY FIELD BOO BIRDS.

REDS BEAT WRITER EARL LAWSON REPORT-ED THAT JOE WAS A "CINCH TO BE WEAR-ING A DIFFERENT UNIFORM NEXT YEAR."

ON SEPT. 29 ROBINSON HIT HIS 29TH HR...OVER THE CROSLEY FIELD SCORE-BOARD!

ROBBY RALLIED IN THE SECOND HALF OF THE SEASON TO FINISH AT .297 WITH 31 HOME RUNS...[31]

...BUT COMBINED, HE, PINSON, AND BELL DROVE IN 118 FEWER RUNS IN 1960 THAN 1959.[32]

THE REDS TOTAL OF 67 WINS WAS THEIR LOWEST SINCE 1950.

LED BY N.L. MVP DICK GROAT THE PIRATES WON THEIR FIRST PENNANT SINCE 1927. THE YANKEES, LED BY A.L. MVP ROGER MARIS, WON THEIR 10TH PENNANT IN 12 YEARS.

ALTHOUGH THEY WERE HEAVY UNDER-DOGS, THE PIRATES WON THE WORLD SERIES, WHEN 2ND BASEMAN BILL MAZEROSKI HIT A 7TH GAME WALK-OFF HR AT FORBES FIELD AGAINST N.Y.'S BILL TERRY.

A COUPLE OF WEEKS AFTER THE WORLD SERIES GABE PAUL LEFT CINCINNATI TO BECOME G.M. OF THE EXPANSION HOUSTON FRANCHISE.

THE REDS REPLACED PAUL WITH BILL DEWITT, WHOSE FIRST TRADE ON DEC. 15 WOULD PAY HUGE DIVIDENDS.[33]

IN A 3-TEAM DEAL THE REDS SENT ROY McMILLAN TO MILWAUKEE FOR PITCHERS JOEY JAY AND JUAN PIZARRO...

...AND THEN SWAPPED PIZARRO AND CAL McLISH TO THE CHICAGO WHITE SOX FOR 3RD BASEMAN GENE FREESE.[34]

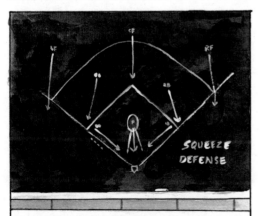

HUTCH ANNOUNCED THAT HE WAS GOING TO HAVE NIGHT SCHOOL FOR THE REDS IN THE SPRING OF 1961, ...

...AND IN JANUARY JOE NUXHALL WAS TRADED AWAY. HE LATER RETURNED TO THE REDS BUT WOULD ALWAYS RUE MISSING THE '61 SEASON.

111

The desk clerk greeted me with a grin and a handshake.

"We've got a convention here," he said. "For you guys we have rooms. For anybody else, no. We're jammed. They're having a tough time finding a room for your party. Hutch is looking for one now."

He found one.

—The end of *Pennant Race* by Jim Brosnan

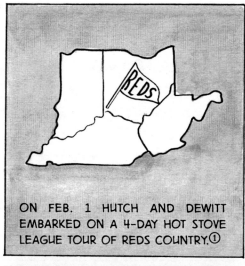

ON FEB. 1 HUTCH AND DEWITT EMBARKED ON A 4-DAY HOT STOVE LEAGUE TOUR OF REDS COUNTRY.①

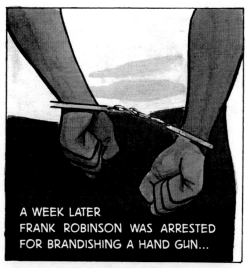

A WEEK LATER
FRANK ROBINSON WAS ARRESTED FOR BRANDISHING A HAND GUN...

...AT AN EMPLOYEE OF SIXTY SECOND HAMBURGERS IN CINCINNATI.

ALTHOUGH ROBINSON WAS LET OFF WITH A $250 FINE, ...

...SOME REDS FANS WERE ANGRY AND WISHED TO SEE HIM TRADED.

HUTCH'S FAITH THAT ROBINSON WOULD USE THE INCIDENT AS A LEARNING EXPERIENCE...

115

...WAS BORNE OUT, AS THE YOUNG MAN GREW UP IN A HURRY AND SET OUT TO REDEEM HIMSELF ON THE DIAMOND.

WHEN THE REDS REPORTED TO SPRING TRAINING IN TAMPA...

...THEY WERE CHAGRINED TO DISCOVER THAT HUTCH HAD HIRED AN EX-PRO FOOTBALL COACH TO BE THE TEAM'S CONDITIONING COACH.②

COACH DOUGLAS'S DAILY WORKOUTS COMBINED WITH HUTCH'S NIGHT CLASSES LEFT LITTLE TIME FOR THE USUAL SPRING FRIVOLITIES.

SECOND BASE APPEARED TO BE THE REDS' WEAKEST POSITION...

...AND JOURNEYMAN JIM BAUMER EVENTUALLY WON THE JOB.

WALLY POST AND GUS BELL WERE ALSO COMPETING FOR AN OUTFIELD SPOT.

"THE JOB IS THERE. THEY CAN FIGHT IT OUT. I WISH EACH OF THEM GOOD LUCK," SAID HUTCH.

THE REDS LOST 8 OF THEIR 1ST 11 GRAPEFRUIT LEAGUE GAMES, AND AFTER A 14-5 LOSS ON MAR. 20, HUTCH BLEW HIS STACK. "WE'RE PLAYING THE WORST BASEBALL I'VE EVER SEEN," HE SAID. "I RANT AND RAVE AND NOTHING HAPPENS. IT'S AS IF THEY JUST DON'T CARE."

HUTCH THREATENED TO START LEVYING FINES BUT ALSO TRIED TO CONVINCE HIS YOUNG PLAYERS THAT THEY WERE BETTER THAN THEY REALIZED.

MAR. 28 WAS A SAD DAY FOR REDS FANS AS OWNER POWEL CROSLEY DIED OF A HEART ATTACK.

CROSLEY OWNED THE CLUB FOR 27 YEARS AND HAD KEPT THE REDS FROM LEAVING CINCINNATI DURING THE DEPRESSION.

AS OPENING DAY 1961 APPROACHED, LITTLE WAS EXPECTED OF THE REDS.

IN FACT, 168 OF 234 WRITERS POLLED PREDICTED THE REDS WOULD FINISH IN SIXTH PLACE AGAIN.[3]

HOWEVER, HUTCH KNEW THAT THE TEAM WAS MUCH IMPROVED, ESPECIALLY WITH THE ADDITIONS OF FREESE, JAY, A STRAPPING ROOKIE PITCHER NAMED KEN HUNT, AND COLEMAN.[4]

ONE OF THE BIG BATS THAT GOT THE REDS OFF TO A GOOD START, THREE STRAIGHT WINS, BELONGED TO STRONGMAN WALLY POST. HE HIT A 3-RUN HR ON OPENING DAY AND A DOUBLE, TRIPLE, AND HR TWO DAYS LATER IN ST. LOUIS. HIS MONSTROUS SHOT AT BUSCH STADIUM WOULD HAVE GONE 560 FEET HAD IT NOT HIT A SIGN ATOP THE SCOREBOARD 90 FEET ABOVE THE FIELD, 410 FEET FROM HOME PLATE. "THE BALL STILL HAD JUICE IN IT WHEN IT HIT THE SIGN," MARVELED HUTCH.

AFTER A 2-12 START BAUMER WAS BENCHED IN FAVOR OF ELIO CHACON...

...WHO PLAYED WELL UNTIL A KNEE INJURY SIDELINED HIM FOR 2 WEEKS.

HUTCH MOVED SS KASKO TO SECOND AND GAVE LEO CARDENAS A SHOT AT SS, ...⑤

...A COMBINATION WHICH WORKED FINE UNTIL A FOOT INJURY SENT KASKO TO THE BENCH AFTER THE GAME ON APR. 23.

AFTER THE REDS LOST THEIR 4TH STRAIGHT (SCORING 5 RUNS TOTAL), HUTCH MADE THE TEAM PLAY AN INTRA-SQUAD GAME UNTIL DARK.⑥

"THIS ISN'T A PUNISHMENT," SAID HUTCH, WHO ALSO PERFORMED A BED CHECK THAT NIGHT.

A FEW DAYS LATER HUTCH GOT HELP AT SECOND WHEN HE WAS RE-UNITED WITH DON BLASINGAME.

THE REDS ACQUIRED THE BLAZER AND 2 OTHER PLAYERS FROM S.F. FOR ED BAILEY.

BOB PURKEY'S 4-2 WIN ON APR. 30 STOPPED THE REDS' LOSING STREAK OF 8...

...AND STARTED A 9-GAME WINNING STREAK WHICH BOOSTED THE TEAM FROM LAST TO 2ND PLACE.

ONE REDS HITTER NOT SLUMPING WAS "GOOD HIT, NO FIELD" JERRY LYNCH, WHO SLUGGED HIS 3RD PINCH HIT HR OF THE YOUNG SEASON ON APR. 26. HUTCH, WHO CALLED LYNCH "THE GREATEST PINCH HITTER I'VE EVER SEEN," HAD SUPREME CONFIDENCE IN THE RESERVE OUTFIELDER AND TRIED TO GET HIM AS MANY AT BATS AS POSSIBLE. JERRY WOULD BAT .315 (9TH BEST IN THE N.L.) WITH 13 HOME RUNS FOR THE SEASON IN 96 GAMES.

GREAT PITCHING AND COMEBACK VICTORIES BECAME THE TEAM'S TRADEMARK.⑦

FOR INSTANCE, ON MAY 5 THE REDS SCORED 4 RUNS IN THE 9TH TO TIE THE BRAVES AND WON THE GAME 6–5 IN THE 12TH.

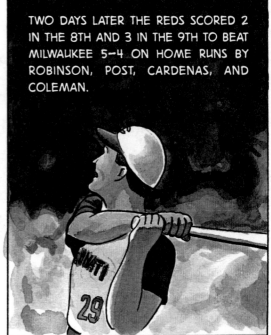

TWO DAYS LATER THE REDS SCORED 2 IN THE 8TH AND 3 IN THE 9TH TO BEAT MILWAUKEE 5–4 ON HOME RUNS BY ROBINSON, POST, CARDENAS, AND COLEMAN.

AFTER THREE LOSSES IN WHICH THE REDS DID NOT SCORE HIM A SINGLE RUN, JOEY JAY NOTCHED HIS FIRST WIN FOR CINCINNATI WITH A ONE-HITTER AGAINST THE PHILLIES ON MAY 4. THIS SET JAY OFF ON A RUN OF 8 STRAIGHT WINS, AND HE WAS NAMED N.L. PLAYER OF THE MONTH FOR MAY. HE ALSO BECAME A LOYAL BACKER OF HUTCH. "WHEN A MANAGER DISPLAYS THAT KIND OF CONFIDENCE IN YOU, YOU'LL BREAK YOUR BACK FOR HIM," SAID JAY.[8]

AS ALWAYS, HUTCH BACKED HIS PLAYERS TO THE HILT DURING JAY'S FIRST WIN.

WHEN ED VARGO ISSUED A WARNING TO JAY FOR BRUSHING BACK RUEBEN AMARO...

...IN RETALIATION FOR ART MAHAFFEY HAVING BEANED FRANK ROBINSON THE PREVIOUS INNING ...

...HUTCH TOLD VARGO, "IF YOU'RE GOING TO THROW SOMEBODY OUT OF THIS GAME, MAKE IT ME."

VARGO OBLIGED AND THE EJECTION COST HUTCH A $100 FINE, BUT AFTERWARDS HE WAS UNREPENTANT.

"WE'LL CONTINUE TO PROTECT OUR HITTERS," HE SAID.

FOR ALL THE RUN-INS WITH UMPIRES, HUTCH NEVER LET THEM CONTINUE OFF THE FIELD.

HUTCH HAD A FEROCIOUS ARGUMENT WITH VINNIE SMITH, AN OLD WAR BUDDY, IN L.A., ...⑨

...BUT WHEN WORD OF A RELATIVE'S DEATH A FEW DAYS LATER REACHED SMITH IN CINCINNATI, ...

...HUTCH SENT HIS CAR KEYS TO SMITH SO HE COULD DRIVE HIMSELF TO THE AIRPORT.

ON MAY 10 THE REDS SHIPPED BAUMER TO DETROIT FOR DICK GERNERT WHO BECAME A VALUABLE BACKUP AT 1ST.

AS MAY CAME TO A CLOSE, THE REDS' SOMETIMES SHAKY DEFENSE BEGAN TO TIGHTEN.

TWO GREAT CATCHES BY ROBINSON AND ANOTHER BY PINSON HELPED JAY BEAT THE PHILLIES AT CROSLEY 5-4 ON MAY 27.

PHILLIES MANAGER GENE MAUCH CALLED PINSON'S GRAB, WHICH ROBBED CHOO CHOO COLEMAN OF A HR, "THE GREATEST CATCH I'VE EVER SEEN."

THE REDS WENT 20-6 IN MAY AND AFTER TAKING A DOUBLE-HEADER IN S.F. ON MAY 30 MOVED INTO A TIE FOR FIRST PLACE.(10)

THE REDS' SWEEP OF A DOUBLE-HEADER AT PHILADELPHIA ON JUNE 18 GAVE CINCINNATI 12 STRAIGHT WINS OVER THE PHILLIES.

THE PHILLIES WOULD BE THE REDS' PATSIES ALL YEAR, LOSING THE SEASON SERIES 19–3.

DURING THE JUNE 18 SWEEP GENE FREESE WENT 7–8 WITH A TRIPLE AND HR.

FREESE USED HIS "OLE DESTROYER" TO GET BIG HITS FOR THE REDS ALL SEASON.

ON JUNE 26 THE REDS CALLED UP FORMER OHIO STATE CATCHER JOHNNY EDWARDS...

...WHO WOULD SHARE THE BACKSTOP DUTIES THE REST OF THE SUMMER WITH JERRY ZIMMERMAN.

EDWARDS' DEBUT CAME IN A REDS 10–8 WIN IN CHICAGO ON JUNE 27 WHEN HE WAS ONE OF 4...

...CONSECUTIVE PINCH HITTERS USED BY HUTCH TO REACH BASE IN A 5-RUN 7TH INNING RALLY.[11]

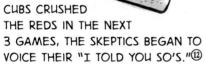

WHEN THE CUBS CRUSHED THE REDS IN THE NEXT 3 GAMES, THE SKEPTICS BEGAN TO VOICE THEIR "I TOLD YOU SO'S."[12]

UNDETERRED, THE REDS WON 10 OF THE NEXT 12 FOR A 5-GAME LEAD AT THE ALL-STAR BREAK.

A BIG HELP IN AMASSING THE LEAD CAME FROM GORDY COLEMAN WHO WENT 8–10 IN A DOUBLE-HEADER SWEEP OF THE BRAVES ON JULY 2.

GORDY'S 3-RUN HR IN THE 13TH OFF WARREN SPAHN WON THE OPENER, ...

127

... A GAME INTERRUPTED BY A 10-MINUTE MELEE STARTED...

...WHEN THE BASERUNNING JIM O'TOOLE TRIED TO SLAP THE BALL OUT OF THE GLOVE OF ED MATHEWS.

DURING THE FRACAS, HUTCH EMBRACED MATHEWS IN A BIG BEAR HUG AND ASKED HIM WHAT HE WAS DOING. "HE TRIED TO KNOCK THE BALL OUT OF MY GLOVE, HUTCH," SAID MATHEWS. "WHAT'D YOU EXPECT HIM TO DO? GIVE YOU A KISS," LAUGHED HUTCH.

IN A POLL OF WRITERS, STILL UNIMPRESSED WITH HUTCH'S BOYS, NO RED WAS DEEMED TO BE WORTHY OF THE ALL-STAR TEAM. THEIR PEERS WHO DID THE VOTING THAT COUNTED PUT ROBINSON AND KASKO ON THE TEAM, ...

...WHILE DANNY MURTAUGH SELECTED PURKEY AND JAY FOR HIS PITCHING STAFF.

VADA PINSON, JIM BROSNAN, AND GORDY COLEMAN ALL DESERVED TO MAKE THE TEAM TOO BUT DID NOT.[13]

CINCINNATIANS FINALLY CAUGHT PENNANT FEVER, AND A SONG PENNED...

Rally Round the Reds

...BY A LOCAL TV CELEBRITY BECAME THE CITY'S UNOFFICIAL SLOGAN.[14]

HUTCH HAD THE SCARE OF HIS LIFE ON JULY 16 WHEN ROBINSON AND PINSON WERE INVOLVED IN A NASTY COLLISION. THE TWO SUPERSTARS SUFFERED ONLY MINOR INJURIES, ...

...BUT WITHIN A WEEK THE REDS' 6-GAME LEAD HAD SHRUNK TO A SINGLE GAME.

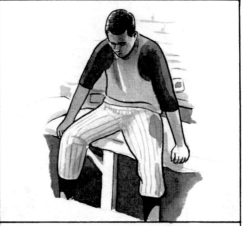

WITH JIM MALONEY AND HOWIE NUNN NURSING SORE ARMS...

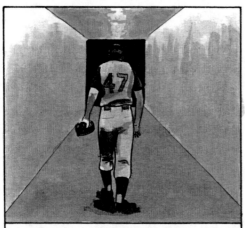

...AND JAY HOOK AND KEN HUNT INCREASINGLY INEFFECTIVE...⑮

...THE REDS NEEDED PITCHING HELP WHICH THEY GOT FROM A 28-YEAR-OLD RETREAD OFF TORONTO'S ROSTER.

KEN JOHNSON WON HIS FIRST START ON JULY 26 AND BECAME A DEPEND-ABLE 4TH STARTER.

FOR BATTING .409 WITH 13 HOME RUNS FRANK ROBINSON WAS NAMED N.L. PLAYER OF THE MONTH FOR JULY.

ROBINSON WAS RECOGNIZED BY WRITERS AROUND THE LEAGUE AS A BONA FIDE MVP CANDIDATE, ...

...BUT THE SCRIBES STILL DID NOT BELIEVE IN THE REDS, REFERRED TO DERISIVELY AS "RAGAMUFFINS."

TRAILING THE DODGERS BY TWO GAMES, THE REDS OPENED A CRUCIAL SERIES IN L.A. ON AUG. 15.

NEITHER THE EXPERTS NOR THE DODGERS WERE PREPARED FOR WHAT HAPPENED NEXT.

THE REDS TOOK THE FIRST GAME 5-2 BEHIND JOEY JAY'S 6-HITTER, ...

...AND THE NEXT DAY BEFORE THE LARGEST CROWD (72,140) TO EVER WATCH THE REDS...

...PURKEY AND O'TOOLE THREW BACK-TO-BACK SHUTOUTS TO PUT CINCINNATI BACK AHEAD IN THE PENNANT RACE BY ONE GAME.[16]

THE DOUBLE SHUTOUT, THE FIRST SUFFERED BY THE DODGERS SINCE 1935, ...[17]

...DEMORALIZED THE DODGERS AND FINALLY CONVINCED A LOT OF DOUBTERS THE REDS WERE "FOR REAL."

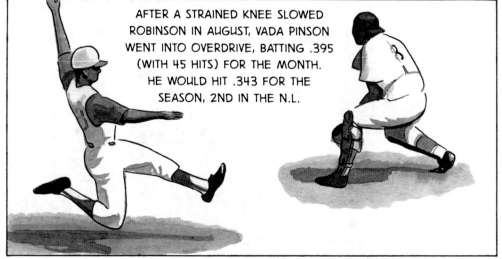

AFTER A STRAINED KNEE SLOWED ROBINSON IN AUGUST, VADA PINSON WENT INTO OVERDRIVE, BATTING .395 (WITH 45 HITS) FOR THE MONTH. HE WOULD HIT .343 FOR THE SEASON, 2ND IN THE N.L.

ON AUG. 23 THE GIANTS HIT 5 HOME RUNS AND SCORED 12 RUNS IN THE 9TH INNING TO EMBARRASS THE REDS 14-0.[18]

AN OUTRAGED HUTCH CLOSED THE CLUBHOUSE TO REPORTERS AND CHEWED OUT THE TEAM.

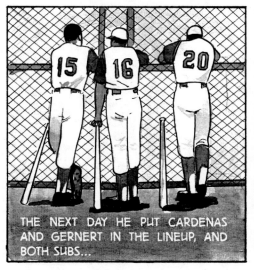

THE NEXT DAY HE PUT CARDENAS AND GERNERT IN THE LINEUP, AND BOTH SUBS...

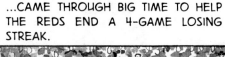

...CAME THROUGH BIG TIME TO HELP THE REDS END A 4-GAME LOSING STREAK.

WITH THE REDS CLINGING TO A 1 1/2 GAME LEAD HUTCH SIGNED A NEW 2-YEAR CONTRACT ON AUG. 26.

AS THE REDS ENJOYED AN OFF DAY AND A 2 1/2 GAME LEAD...

...FRED AND TWO OF HIS COACHES SHOWED UP AT YANKEE STADIUM...[19]

...TO WATCH WHITEY FORD AND MATES TAKE ON THE DETROIT TIGERS.

HUTCH COYLY DENIED HE WAS SCOUTING THE N.L.'S PROBABLE WORLD SERIES OPPONENT, BUT NO ONE BELIEVED HIM.

KEN JOHNSON'S SHUTOUT OF PITTSBURGH ON SEPT. 4 WAS HIS SIXTH WIN DOWN THE STRETCH.[20]

"HE'S GIVEN US A BIG LIFT RIGHT WHEN WE NEEDED IT," SAID HUTCH.

ON SEPT. 13 JOEY JAY WON HIS 20TH GAME OF THE SEASON.

134

THE 1-0 WIN WAS HIS 4TH SHUTOUT OF THE YEAR AND CAME AGAINST HIS FORMER CLUB.

IT ALSO MADE HIM THE FIRST REDS PITCHER TO WIN 20 GAMES SINCE EWELL BLACKWELL IN 1947.

HUTCH'S TWO KNIGHTS ON THE CORNERS CONTINUED TO EXCEL AS THE REDS MOVED EVER CLOSER TO CHECKMATING THE REST OF THE N.L. ON SEPT. 19 GENE FREESE BLASTED A PAIR OF HOME RUNS IN SUPPORT OF O'TOOLE'S 17TH WIN; WHILE GORDY COLEMAN HIT ANOTHER PAIR ON SEPT. 23 TO HELP O'TOOLE WIN HIS 18TH. FREESE AND COLEMAN FINISHED THE YEAR WITH 26 HOME RUNS AND 87 RBI EACH.[21]

ON SEPT. 24 THE REDS ANNOUNCED THEY WERE NO LONGER ACCEPTING APPLICATIONS FOR WORLD SERIES TICKETS. THEY HAD ALREADY RECEIVED MORE THAN 146,000.

ON SEPT. 26 THE REDS PLAYED AT WRIGLEY FIELD, NEEDING ONE WIN TO CLINCH A TIE FOR THE N.L. PENNANT. AFTER 5 THE CUBS LED 3-0, BUT HOME RUNS BY EDWARDS AND ROBINSON TIED IT. IN THE 8TH JERRY LYNCH CRACKED A 2-RUN HR TO PUT THE REDS AHEAD TO STAY, AND AFTER BROSNAN PITCHED THE LAST OF HIS 3 SCORELESS INNINGS IN RELIEF, THE PARTY WAS ON![22]

THE HUNDREDS OF FANS WHO GREETED THE TEAM AT THE
CINCINNATI AIRPORT THAT NIGHT WAS ONLY THE BEGINNING.

MORE THAN 30,000 FANS DESCENDED UPON FOUNTAIN
SQUARE AND INTO THE SURROUNDING DOWNTOWN
STREETS TO WELCOME THE TEAM HOME.

THE BUS CARRYING THE PLAYERS ARRIVED ON THE SCENE AT 9:30, ...

...AND THE DOORS OF THE BUS COULD BARELY BE SQUEEZED OPEN.

HUTCH AND DEWITT ACCEPTED WELL-DESERVED CONGRATULATIONS, ...

...AND HUTCH TOLD ANNOUNCER WAITE HOYT HOW PROUD HE WAS OF THE TEAM.

SOMEBODY PUT DETERGENT INTO THE FOUNTAIN WHICH OVERFLOWED WITH BUBBLES, ...

...AS THE FANS FOLLOWED THE DODGERS—PIRATES GAME ON TRANSITOR RADIOS.

WHEN LOUDSPEAKERS ANNOUNCED AT 10:00 THAT THE PIRATE WIN MADE THE REDS N.L. CHAMPS...㉓

...THE WHOLE CITY BROKE INTO CELEBRATION.

LATER AT A TEAM PARTY HELD AT THE NETHERLAND HOTEL...

HUTCH AMAZED HIS PLAYERS BY BEAUTIFULLY SINGING HIS FAVORITE SONG.

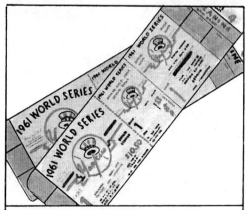

EVEN BEFORE THE PARTY ENDED THOUGH, HUTCH WAS THINKING AHEAD, TO OCTOBER 4.

IN ITS OCT. 4 EDITION *THE SPORTING NEWS* PRAISED HUTCH FOR THE JOB HE HAD DONE IN THE 1961 SEASON.[24]

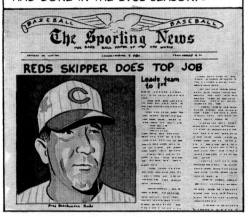

STILL, THE YANKEES, MANAGED BY RALPH HOUK, WERE BIG FAVORITES TO WIN THE WORLD SERIES.

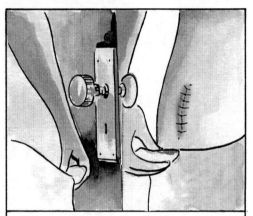

AFTER ALL, THEY HAD THE TWO BEST SLUGGERS IN THE A.L.: MICKEY MANTLE AND ROGER MARIS, WHO HAD JUST BROKEN BABE RUTH'S RECORD OF HOME RUNS IN A SINGLE SEASON.[25]

WHEN HE LEARNED THAT A HIP INJURY WOULD KEEP MANTLE OUT OF GAME ONE, ...[26]

...HUTCH SAID HE WAS SORRY. "WE WANT TO BEAT THEM AT THEIR BEST," HE SAID.

THE 1961 WORLD SERIES WAS THE FOURTH FOR THE REDS; THE 23RD FOR THE YANKEES. WHILE THE REDS WOULD PLAY BEFORE STANDING ROOM ONLY CROWDS IN CINCINNATI, GAMES ONE AND TWO IN NEW YORK WERE NOT SELL OUTS.

WHITEY FORD DOMINATED GAME ONE AS HE SHUT OUT THE REDS ON 2 HITS.

HE GOT ALL THE RUNS HE NEEDED ON SOLO HOME RUNS BY ELLIE HOWARD AND BILL SKOWRON.

"THERE'S NOT MUCH I CAN SAY. JUST GIVE WHITEY FORD A LOT OF CREDIT," MUSED HUTCH.

JOEY JAY'S 4-HITTER EVENED THE SERIES THE NEXT DAY.

THE REDS SCORED 1ST IN THE TOP OF THE 4TH ON COLEMAN'S 2-RUN HR, ...

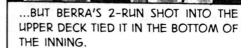

...BUT BERRA'S 2-RUN SHOT INTO THE UPPER DECK TIED IT IN THE BOTTOM OF THE INNING.

THE GAME-WINNING RUN WAS SCORED IN THE 5TH WHEN
ELIO CHACON DASHED HOME ON A SHORT PASSED BALL.

AS THE HAPPY HEROES MUGGED FOR
PHOTOGRAPHERS, ...

...HUTCH ASKED SARCASTICALLY,
"WHERE'S THE EXPERT WHO SAID N.Y.
WOULD WIN IN 3 GAMES?"

WHILE CINCINNATI FANS WERE PAINTING
THE TOWN RED, THE BALLCLUB GAVE CROSLEY
FIELD A FRESH COAT OF WHITE PAINT.

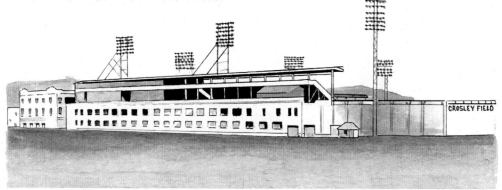

GAME 3, AT CROSLEY, WAS A PITCHERS' DUEL BETWEEN PURKEY AND BILL STAFFORD...

...THAT WAS KNOTTED 2–2 IN THE 8TH ON A HR BY JOHNNY BLANCHARD...

...AND DECIDED IN FAVOR OF N.Y. 3–2 WHEN ROGER MARIS, HITLESS TO THAT POINT, HOMERED IN THE TOP OF THE 9TH INNING.[27]

N.Y.'S FIRST RUN SCORED WHEN ROBINSON GOT A LATE START ON A SHALLOW POP FLY...

...AND THEN BUMPED INTO CHACON, CAUSING HIM TO DROP THE BALL.

EVER PROTECTIVE OF HIS PLAYERS, HUTCH REFUSED TO BLAME ROBINSON FOR THE LOSS.

IN GAME 4 WHITEY FORD SHUT OUT THE REDS AGAIN, FOR 5 INNINGS,...[28]

...AND BROKE BABE RUTH'S WORLD SERIES RECORD FOR CONSECUTIVE SCORELESS INNINGS PITCHED.

JIM COATES STIFLED THE REDS THE REST OF THE DAY FOR A 7-0 N.Y. WIN.

MICKEY MANTLE WITHDREW FROM THE SERIES AFTER GETTING HIS FIRST AND ONLY HIT,...[29]

...BUT BOBBY RICHARDSON AND SKOWRON WITH 3 HITS EACH PICKED UP THE SLACK.[30]

145

AFTER FOUR GAMES 3 OF THE REDS' BEST HITTERS HAD A TOTAL OF 2 HITS.[31]

PRIOR TO GAME FIVE VENERABLE GROUNDSKEEPER MATTY SCHWAB...

...THREW OUT THE FIRST PITCH. IT WAS THE HIGHLIGHT OF THE DAY FOR THE REDS.

AN INJURY RELEGATED BERRA TO THE BENCH NEXT TO MANTLE, ...

...BUT IT HARDLY MATTERED, AS SUBS BLANCHARD AND HECTOR LOPEZ...

...BATTERED REDS PITCHING FOR 5 HITS, 2 HOME RUNS, AND 8 RBI.

REDS STARTER JOEY JAY DIDN'T SUR-
VIVE THE FIRST INNING, AND TRYING TO
STEM THE N.Y. ONSLAUGHT, ...

...HUTCH USED 7 MORE PITCHERS, A
WORLD SERIES RECORD.

THE REDS DID KNOCK OUT N.Y. STARTER
RALPH TERRY, BUT BUD DALEY ALLOWED
NO EARNED RUNS OVER THE FINAL $6^2/_3$
INNINGS TO SEAL THE YANKEES' 13–5 WIN.

WHEN IT WAS ALL OVER, HUTCH TOLD
HOUK: "WELL, WE GAVE YOU A BATTLE
FOR A WHILE." "THAT YOU DID," SAID
HOUK, "AND CONGRATULATIONS ON
YOUR GREAT YEAR."[32]

CHAPTER 6

A Clean Bill of Health, 1962–1964

"We saw Hutch go from 220 pounds to 140 pounds with the cancer and he never once complained. Tough. Really tough. More than baseball tough. He was a man."

Pete Rose in *Pete Rose: My Story* by Pete Rose and Roger Kahn

IN THE REDS' FIRST GAME EVER AGAINST THE N.Y. METS ELLIS SHOWED HE WASN'T READY FOR THE M.L. EITHER.

SAMMY GAVE UP ONLY ONE HIT IN 5 INNINGS BUT HE ALSO WALKED 11.⑨

ROBINSON DIDN'T HIT HIS FIRST HR UNTIL APRIL 27, AND THE REDS ENDED THE MONTH AT 8–11.

ON APRIL 22 FRANK ROBINSON RECEIVED HIS N.L. MVP AWARD FOR 1961. IRONICALLY, HE WENT HIT-LESS IN THE GAME THAT NIGHT AND BATTED ONLY .186 FOR THE MONTH OF APRIL.⑩

ON MAY 6 THE METS SENT THE REDS NATIVE CINCINNAT-IAN DON ZIMMER, WHO GOT 3 STRAIGHT PINCH HITS FOR HUTCH.⑪

LED BY JOEY JAY AND BOB PURKEY, WHO WAS OFF TO THE BEST START OF HIS CAREER, THE
REDS BEGAN TO JELL IN MAY. AFTER WINNING 11 OF 13 THEY MOVED INTO FOURTH PLACE
ON MAY 16. ON MAY 13 PURKEY RAN HIS RECORD TO 6-0 WITH A 6-4 WIN OVER THE
PIRATES. BEFORE THE GAME THE REDS RECEIVED THEIR N.L. CHAMPIONS RINGS AND HUTCH
WAS PRESENTED WITH A 1961 PENNANT FLAG.

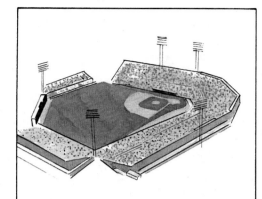

ON MAY 23 THE REDS LOST THEIR FIRST EVER GAME IN HOUSTON, BUT THEY BOUNCED BACK...⑫

...THE NEXT NIGHT AS JAY'S SIX-HIT SHUTOUT IGNITED ANOTHER WINNING STREAK.⑬

WITH HELP FROM JOHN KLIPPSTEIN AND MARTY KEOUGH THE REDS WON 9 OF 10 AND TOOK POSSESSION OF THIRD PLACE ON JUNE 1.⑭

ON JULY 8 THE REDS SWEPT A DAY-NIGHT DOUBLE-HEADER FROM HOUSTON AT CROSLEY FIELD...⑮

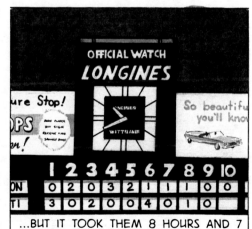

...BUT IT TOOK THEM 8 HOURS AND 7 MINUTES TO DO IT, A M.L. RECORD FOR TIME PLAYED.

ON JULY 10 HUTCH MANAGED THE N.L. TO A 3-1 WIN IN THE 32ND ALL-STAR GAME.[16]

MAURY WILLS, WHO RAN THE A.L. RAGGED, WAS THE STAR OF THE GAME.[17]

JOE NUXHALL RE-JOINED THE REDS IN MID-JULY AND PITCHED EFFECTIVELY THE REST OF THE SEASON.[18]

AFTER A 14-3 HOME STAND, THE REDS WENT ON A CRITICAL 9-GAME ROAD TRIP TO NEW YORK AND HOUSTON.

THE REDS LOST A DOUBLE-HEADER TO THE LOWLY METS ON AUGUST 4, 9-1 AND 3-2.[19]

A FRANK THOMAS HR ENDED THE SECOND GAME IN THE BOTTOM OF THE 14TH INNING.

AFTERWARDS, A DISTRAUGHT AND FUMING HUTCH SAT IN THE DUGOUT, ALONE.

HE SENT WORD THAT HE WANTED THE REDS' CLUBHOUSE COMPLETELY EMPTY IN 15 MINUTES.

REDS PLAYERS SHOWERED, DRESSED, AND VACATED THE VISITORS' CLUBHOUSE AT THE POLO GROUNDS IN RECORD TIME.

THE REDS RECOVERED AND PLAYED WELL BUT JUST COULDN'T KEEP PACE...

...WITH THE GIANTS AND DODGERS, WHO TIED FOR THE N.L. PENNANT.[20]

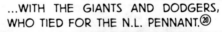

THE REDS CLINCHED 3RD PLACE ON SEPT. 25 WITH A 2-1 WIN OVER PITTSBURGH. IT WAS THE 23RD WIN OF THE YEAR FOR PURKEY, WHO COMBINED WITH JAY (21-14) TO FORM THE REDS' 1ST 20-WIN COMBO SINCE 1940.

AS FOR FRANK ROBINSON, AFTER HE TURNED THE PAGE ON APRIL, HE PUT TOGETHER ANOTHER SPECTACULAR SEASON. HE HIT .342 WITH 39 HOME RUNS AND 136 RBI, AND LOST THE BATTING TITLE TO TOMMY DAVIS BY ONLY 4 POINTS.[21]

THE REDS' FAILURE TO REPEAT WAS DIS-APPOINTING, BUT HUTCH TOOK SOME CONSOLATION...[22]

...IN THE FACT THAT SONS RICK AND JACK PLAYED FOR THE TEAM THAT WON THE AMERICAN LEGION CHAMPIONSHIP FOR THE STATE OF FLORIDA.

IN JANUARY AN OPTIMISTIC HUTCH SAID, "WE'RE GOOD ENOUGH TO WIN THE PENNANT IN 1963."[23]

AND FOR ONCE, A LOT OF THE EXPERTS LIKED THE REDS' CHANCES TOO.[24]

THE SURPRISE OF SPRING TRAINING WAS A FRECKLE-FACED DYNAMO NAMED PETE ROSE...[25]

...WHO SURPRISED HUTCH WITH HIS SPIRIT, DESIRE, AND HUSTLE...

...AND BEAT OUT DON BLASINGAME FOR THE JOB AT SECOND BASE.

AFTER ROSE STARTED 3-23 HUTCH BENCHED HIM FOR A WEEK.[26]

159

HUTCH PUT ROSE BACK INTO THE LINEUP ON APRIL 27 AND DIDN'T HAVE TO WORRY ABOUT HIM AGAIN. "CHARLEY HUSTLE" BEAT THE OPPOSITION EVERY WAY POSSIBLE, EVEN SCORING THE WINNING RUN ON JULY 3 ON A WILD PICKOFF THROW TO FIRST.[27]

HUTCH HAD PLENTY OF OTHER PROBLEMS THOUGH: BOB PURKEY'S SORE ARM...[28]

...JOEY JAY'S HARD LUCK AND INEF- FECTIVENESS, ...[29]

...AND THE NEAR SEASON-LONG SLUMP AT BAT BY REDS HITTERS.[30]

ON JULY 15 THE REDS LEFT 18 MEN ON BASE, ...

...AND SCORED THE WINNING RUN IN THE 12TH ON A BASE ON BALLS.(31)

LEO CARDENAS WAS GOING SO BAD THAT HE ONCE SHOWERED IN HIS UNIFORM...

...AND LATER PACKED HIS BAGS TO GO HOME IN THE MIDDLE OF A GAME.(32)

IN AN EFFORT TO TURN THE TEAM AROUND HUTCH STARTED FINING PLAYERS FOR MENTAL MISTAKES, ...

WORKOUT AT 11 A.M. MONDAY EVERYONE!

...HELD PRACTICES ON SCHEDULED OFF DAYS, ...

...AND GOT HIMSELF EXCUSED FROM A NUMBER OF GAMES FOR INDELICATELY DEFENDING HIS TEAM'S INTERESTS.(33)

THE REDS' SLIM CHANCES OF STAGING A LATE-SEASON RALLY WERE DASHED BY INJURIES TO
KEY PLAYERS. FRANK ROBINSON, ALREADY HAVING AN OFF YEAR, WAS BADLY SPIKED WHILE
SLIDING INTO SECOND ON SEPT. 10, AND A WEEK LATER GENE FREESE BROKE HIS WRIST. THE
REDS LIMPED HOME IN FIFTH PLACE, 13 GAMES BEHIND THE CHAMPION DODGERS. THEY
WOULDN'T HAVE FINISHED THAT HIGH IF NOT FOR THE PITCHING OF JOE NUXHALL, JOHN
TSITOURIS, AND, ESPECIALLY, JIM MALONEY, WHO BLOSSOMED INTO AN ACE STRIKEOUT ARTIST.
MALONEY WON 23 GAMES AND FANNED A TEAM RECORD 265 BATTERS IN 250 INNINGS.(34)

ON OCT. 25 HUTCH ATTENDED A DINNER IN FRESNO, CALIFORNIA, IN HONOR OF JIM MALONEY.

HE PRAISED HIS YOUNG STAR AND PROMISED THAT THE REDS WOULD BE CONTENDERS IN 1964. [35]

HUTCH ALSO ATTENDED THE MINOR LEAGUE MEETINGS IN SAN DIEGO IN EARLY DECEMBER.

THERE HE LAUGHED OFF YOGI BERRA'S SUGGESTION THAT THE REDS TRADE JOHNNY EDWARDS TO THE YANKEES. [36]

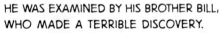

ON CHRISTMAS EVE HUTCH COMPLAINED OF SORENESS IN HIS NECK.

HE WAS EXAMINED BY HIS BROTHER BILL, WHO MADE A TERRIBLE DISCOVERY.

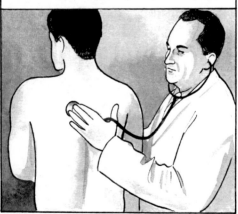

163

AS REDS OWNER BILL DEWITT ANNOUNCED: HUTCH WAS SUFFERING FROM CHEST CANCER, ...(37)

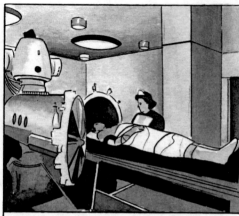

...AND WAS SCHEDULED TO SPEND THE NEXT TWO MONTHS IN SEATTLE RECEIVING RADIATION TREATMENTS.(38)

ON JAN. 5 HUTCH HELD A PRESS CON-FERENCE IN THE OFFICE OF HIS OLD PAL, DEWEY SORIANO.

"NATURALLY, IT'S A SHOCK TO LEARN SOMETHING LIKE THIS," HUTCH SAID. "IT'S LIKE HAVING A RUG JERKED OUT FROM UNDER YOU."(39)

HUTCH CANCELLED A COACHING CLINIC TRIP TO EUROPE WITH ROBIN ROBERTS AND OTHER COLLEAGUES, ...(40)

...AND RENTED A HOUSE IN SEATTLE WITH PATSY, PATTY, AND JOE.

HUTCH GAVE UP SMOKING AND BETWEEN TREATMENTS PLAYED A LOT OF GOLF.

THE BEAR MELLOWED CONSIDERABLY AND NO LONGER BROKE GOLF CLUBS.

ON FEB. 4 ONE OF HUTCH'S DOCTORS HAD GOOD NEWS: THE TUMOR WAS SHRINKING. 41

WHEN HUTCH SHOWED UP FOR SPRING TRAINING, HE SAID HE'D BEEN GIVEN A CLEAN BILL OF HEALTH. 42

BUT THAT WAS A FIB AND HE REMAINED A VERY SICK MAN, ...

...WHO NEEDED A GOLF CART TO SHUTTLE BETWEEN THE REDS' PRACTICE FIELDS.

THE REDS WERE BEATEN ON OPENING DAY, APRIL 13, BY HOUSTON'S KEN JOHNSON. THE COLTS PITCHER DEDICATED THE WIN TO HIS FORMER ROOMMATE, JIM UMBRICHT, WHO'D DIED OF CANCER APRIL 8.[43]

AFTER THE GAME HUTCH FLEW BACK TO SEATTLE FOR ANOTHER EXAMINATION.[44]

RE-JOINING THE REDS ON APRIL 16 IN L.A., HUTCH PRETENDED ALL WAS WELL, BUT OTHERS KNEW BETTER.[45]

ON MAY 12 SEVERAL PLAYERS SAW HUTCH HAVE DIFFICULTY HANGING HIS JACKET IN THE DUGOUT, ...

...AND THAT NIGHT FRED ASKED BOB PRINCE TO "FIND ME A DOCTOR WHO'LL KEEP HIS MOUTH SHUT AND GIVE ME SOMETHING TO KILL THE PAIN."

WITH GORDY COLEMAN SLUMPING HUTCH PLANNED TO PLAY DERON JOHNSON AT 1ST BASE.(46)

THE PAPERS THE NEXT MORNING ANNOUNCED THE MOVE AND MADE HUTCH CHANGE HIS MIND.

"I CAN'T HUMILIATE A GUY WHO TRIES AS HARD AS GORDY," SAID HUTCH.

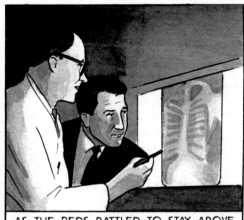

AS THE REDS BATTLED TO STAY ABOVE .500 HUTCH FLEW TO SEATTLE FOR ANOTHER CHECKUP ON JUNE 7.

FIRST BASE COACH DICK SISLER MAN-AGED THE TEAM UNTIL HUTCH RETURNED ON JUNE 9.

CONTINUING TO LIVE AND WORK AS THOUGH NOTHING WERE WRONG, HUTCH STARTED SMOKING AGAIN IN HOUSTON.

HE EVEN UTTERED A RARE COMPLAINT: "DAMMIT, EARL (BEAT WRITER EARL LAWSON), I'M SO SKINNY IT HURTS JUST SITTING DOWN."

IN MID-JULY THE REDS WERE IN THIRD PLACE, CHASING THE HOT PHILADELPHIA PHILLIES. [47]

ON JULY 27 HUTCH, SUFFERING FROM BACK PAINS, ENTERED A CINCINNATI HOSPITAL.

THAT NIGHT HE SENT THE TEAM A CONGRATULATORY TELEGRAM FOR THEIR 4-2 WIN IN MILWAUKEE. [48]

HUTCH RE-JOINED THE TEAM FOR A HOME STAND- OPENING DOUBLE- HEADER AGAINST THE BRAVES ON AUG. 4, ...

...BUT HE LASTED ONLY 7 INNINGS. HE SPENT THE REST OF THE NIGHT IN DEWITT'S ROOFTOP BOX. [49]

168

THE LAST NIGHT OF THE HOME STAND FELL ON HUTCH'S BIRTHDAY, AUGUST 12. HUTCH'S 45TH
BIRTHDAY CELEBRATION WAS A SAD OCCASION AS MOST FANS REALIZED THAT THE GAUNT
MANAGER, WHO'D ALREADY LOST 25 POUNDS, WAS DYING. FRED REQUESTED A LEAVE OF
ABSENCE, SAYING, "I INTEND TO TAKE A SHORT VACATION AND SPEND IT WITH MY FAMILY
IN CINCINNATI. I'LL SEE HOW I FEEL WHEN THE TEAM GETS BACK." FRED WENT BACK
INTO THE HOSPITAL, AND SISLER TOOK OVER AS "ACTING MANAGER."⑤⓪

AFTER RECEIVING A VISIT FROM CASEY STENGEL, HUTCH CHECKED OUT OF THE HOSPITAL ON AUG. 27, ...

...BUT HE RETURNED ON A DAILY BASIS FOR FURTHER TREATMENTS.

ON SEPT. 21 THE REDS BEAT THE PHILLIES 1-0 WHEN ROOKIE CHICO RUIZ STOLE HOME IN THE 6TH INNING.(51)

JIM O'TOOLE AND ROOKIE BILLY McCOOL ALSO PITCHED THE REDS TO WINS OVER PHILLY, ...(52)

...AND AFTER THE REDS SWEPT A 5-GAME SERIES IN N.Y., THEY CAME HOME IN FIRST PLACE WITH 5 GAMES LEFT TO PLAY.(53)

170

ON SEPT. 29 THE REDS FELL INTO A TIE FOR FIRST WITH ST. LOUIS AFTER LOSING 2-0 TO PITTSBURGH.[54]

THE REDS LOST THE NEXT NIGHT TOO, 1-0 IN 16 INNINGS ON A SQUEEZE BUNT.[55]

AFTER THE REDS SALVAGED THE FINALE OF THE SERIES WITH PITTSBURGH, THEIR SEASON CAME DOWN TO THE LAST 2 GAMES OF THE YEAR AGAINST THE PHILLIES, SUFFERING ONE OF THE WORST COLLAPSES IN BASEBALL HISTORY.[56]

HUTCH WAS ON HAND FOR ALL 5 OF THESE GAMES, SAYING GOODBYE TO FRIENDS AND FORMER RIVALS...

...AND WATCHING THE GAMES, INCLUDING THE 16-INNING MARATHON, IN DEWITT'S PRIVATE BOX.

ON OCT. 2 THE REDS LED 3–0 AFTER 7 BUT LOST 4–3 TO THE PHILLIES.(57)

FULL OF ADMIRATION FOR HUTCH'S COURAGE, PHILLIES MANAGER GENE MAUCH PAID TRIBUTE TO HIM, SAYING, "HE SHOWED US HOW TO LIVE. NOW HE'S SHOWING US HOW TO DIE."

WHEN THE PHILLIES THEN BEAT THE REDS 10–0 AND ST. LOUIS BEAT N.Y. 11–5, IT WAS ALL OVER.(58)

ST. LOUIS WON THE PENNANT BY ONE GAME, AND THE REDS AND PHILLIES TIED FOR SECOND.(59)

IN THE QUIET REDS CLUBHOUSE HUTCH SHARED THE DISAPPOINTMENT OF HIS PLAYERS.

REFERRING TO HUTCH, DICK SISLER SAID, "I WISH WE COULD HAVE WON THE PENNANT FOR THAT GENTLEMAN THERE."

IN A RASPY VOICE, A TIRED HUTCH SAID, "I WISH THE PLAYERS COULD HAVE WON IT FOR THEMSELVES."

HUTCH AND FAMILY RETURNED TO THEIR GULF COAST HOME ON ANNA MARIE ISLAND, ...

FRED HUTCHINSON
104 75TH ST.
ANNA MARIE ISLAND, FLA

Mr. William O DeWitt
Cincinnati Reds
415 Union Center Buil
Cincinnati, Ohio

...AND FROM THERE ON OCT. 19 FRED OFFICIALLY RESIGNED AS MANAGER OF THE CINCINNATI REDS.

ON MONDAY NOV. 9 HUTCH WAS ADMITTED TO BRADENTON'S MANATEE MEMORIAL HOSPITAL.

HOSPITAL PERSONNEL ONLY

HE WAS PLACED ON THE CRITICAL LIST ON WEDNESDAY, ...

...AND ON THURSDAY NOV. 12, AT 3:58 AM WITH
HIS WIFE AND CHILDREN BY HIS SIDE, HE DIED.

THE NEXT DAY THE CARACUS LIONS WERE IN THE DOMINICAN REPUBLIC
ON THEIR WAY TO A GAME IN SANTO DOMINGO. ⑥⓪

THEIR MANAGER, REGGIE OTERO, WAS
LISTENING TO THE RADIO.

HE HEARD THE NEWS ABOUT HIS BEST
FRIEND, AND TEARS RAN DOWN HIS
FACE.

*"I'm humbled and honored to receive this award.
We are indebted to the Hutch. Being associated with this
prestigious award is all the more satisfying because it comes
from such a great family, especially the late Dr. Bill Hutchinson."*

Seattle Mariners pitcher Jamie Moyer, winner of the 2003 Hutch Award

HUTCH'S DEATH HIT A LOT OF PEOPLE HARD, ESPECIALLY BILL DEWITT WHO SAID, "UNDERNEATH HIS GRUFF EXTERIOR HE WAS VERY SOFT-HEARTED, GENTEEL AND ONE OF THE MOST LOYAL PERSONS I'VE EVER HAD THE PLEASURE TO KNOW." ①

JIM O'TOOLE SAID, "HUTCH WAS LIKE A FATHER TO ME. I HAD MORE RESPECT FOR HIM THAN ANY OTHER MAN I'VE MET IN BASEBALL." ②

AND MAYOR BACHRACH SENT PATSY CONDOLENCES "ON BEHALF OF THE CITIZENS OF CINCINNATI AND ALL CINCINNATI REDS FANS EVERYWHERE."

ON SATURDAY A FUNERAL SERVICE WAS HELD FOR HUTCH ON THE ISLAND, ...③

...AND HIS BODY WAS LATER FLOWN TO SEATTLE FOR BURIAL. ④

177

THE REDS IMMEDIATELY RETIRED
HUTCH'S UNIFORM NUMBER, ...⑤

...AND WHICH IS STILL ON DISPLAY
TODAY AT GREAT AMERICAN BALLPARK.

...AN HONOR WHICH WAS SYMBOLIZED
AT RIVERFRONT STADIUM...

CINCINNATI HALL OF FAME

FRED HUTCHINSON
INDUCTED JULY 15, 1965
MANAGER REDS JULY 8 1959
OCTOBER 19 1964
MANAGER REDS TO 1961 PENNANT
A GREAT COMPETITOR
A GREAT MANAGER
A GREAT MAN

IN 1965 HUTCH WAS
ELECTED TO THE REDS
HALL OF FAME, AND...⑥

SPORT
FEBRUARY 50¢
FRED HUTCHINSON
Man of the Year

I STILL CAN WIN
By Warren Spahn

BEHIND THE
BERRA FIRING

LENNY MOORE
AND HIS
AMAZING
COMEBACK

7 NEW FEATURES
THE SPORT
BONUS REPORT
By OSCAR ROBERTSON
HOW TO BE A
PLAYMAKER
HOW YOU CAN TALK
TO THE STARS

...SPORT MAGAZINE POSTHUMOUSLY
NAMED HIM MAN OF THE YEAR.⑦

TO PERPETUATE FRED'S MEMORY DR. BILL HUTCHINSON CREATED
THE FRED HUTCHINSON CANCER RESEARCH CENTER (FHCRC),
WHOSE MISSION IS "THE ELIMINATION OF CANCER AND RELATED
DISEASES AS CAUSES OF HUMAN SUFFERING AND DEATH."[8]

THREE WINNERS OF THE NOBEL PRIZE
ARE AMONG THE MANY DEDICATED
SCIENTISTS AND DOCTORS...[9]

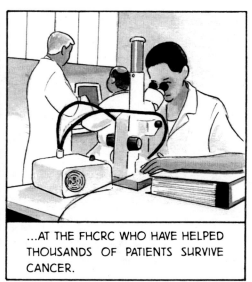

...AT THE FHCRC WHO HAVE HELPED
THOUSANDS OF PATIENTS SURVIVE
CANCER.

IN ADDITION, THREE OF FRED'S FRIENDS, PIRATES BROADCASTER BOB PRINCE, CHICAGO SPORTSWRITER JIM ENRIGHT, AND DAYTON (OH) SPORTS EDITOR RITTER COLLETT, CREATED AN AWARD TO HONOR HIM AND KEEP HIS MEMORY ALIVE.[10]

FRED HUTCHINSON
Award · 1965

HONOR   COURAGE

DEDICATION   MANLINESS

presented to

MICKEY MANTLE

as the baseball player most typifying the courage and character of Fred Hutchinson

This award is made by the Baseball Writers of America and the Major League Broadcasters ... all friends of "Hutch"

THE HUTCH AWARD IS GIVEN ANNUALLY TO THE MAJOR LEAGUE PLAYER WHO BEST EXEMPLIFIES FRED'S CHARACTER AND FIGHTING SPIRIT AND WHO OVERCOMES ANY FORM OF ADVERSITY.[11]

...AND MICKEY HAD GREAT RESPECT FOR HUTCH, HAVING COMPETED AGAINST HIS TEAMS SEVERAL TIMES.

YANKEES GREAT MICKEY MANTLE WAS THE WINNER OF THE FIRST HUTCH AWARD IN 1965. MANTLE WAS CYNICAL ABOUT SOME OF THE MANY AWARDS HE'D RECEIVED BUT NOT THIS ONE.[12]

AFTER ALL, HIS OWN FATHER, MUTT MANTLE, HAD DIED OF CANCER, ...

MANTLE THOUGHT SO HIGHLY OF THE HUTCH AWARD THAT HE EVEN SHOWED UP TO PRESENT THE 1966 AWARD TO DODGERS PITCHING GREAT SANDY KOUFAX.

IN ADDITION TO MANTLE AND KOUFAX, 9 OTHER PLAYERS WHO EVENTUALLY GOT ELECTED TO THE BASEBALL HALL OF FAME HAVE WON THE HUTCH AWARD.[13]

OTHER NOTABLE WINNERS WERE DANNY THOMPSON, WHO WAS DIAGNOSED WITH LEUKEMIA DURING THE 1974 SEASON; ...[14]

...DAVE DRAVECKY, WHO CAME BACK FROM CANCER IN HIS PITCHING ARM; ...[15]

182

...AND JIM ABBOTT, WHO WAS BORN WITHOUT A RIGHT HAND. [16]

IN 2006 BOSTON ROOKIE JON LESTER WAS DIAGNOSED WITH CANCER. [17]

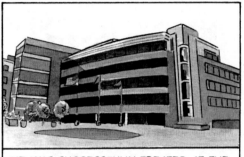

HE WAS SUCCESSFULLY TREATED AT THE FHCRC, AND HE RETURNED TO THE RED SOX IN THE MIDDLE OF THE 2007 SEASON. [18]

ON OCT. 28 LESTER BEAT THE COLORADO ROCKIES TO CLINCH THE 2007 WORLD SERIES FOR BOSTON, ...

...AND ON MAY 19, 2008, HE PITCHED A NO-HITTER AGAINST THE KANSAS CITY ROYALS. [19]

IN LATE 2008 THE HUTCH AWARD CAME FULL CIRCLE
WHEN LESTER BECAME THE FIRST PATIENT OF THE
FRED HUTCHINSON CANCER RESEARCH CENTER TO
WIN THE HUTCH AWARD. NO ONE COULD HAVE BEEN
PROUDER OF JON THAN HUTCH HIMSELF.

APPENDIX: HUTCH AWARD WINNERS

1965 Mickey Mantle, New York Yankees

1966 Sandy Koufax, Los Angeles Dodgers

1967 Carl Yastrzemski, Boston Red Sox

1968 Pete Rose, Cincinnati Reds

1969 Al Kaline, Detroit Tigers

1970 Tony Conigliaro, Boston Red Sox

1971 Joe Torre, St. Louis Cardinals

1972 Bobby Tolan, Cincinnati Reds

1973 John Hiller, Detroit Tigers

1974 Danny Thompson, Minnesota Twins

1975 Gary Nolan, Cincinnati Reds

1976 Tommy John, Los Angeles Dodgers

1977 Willie McCovey, San Francisco Giants

1978 Willie Stargell, Pittsburgh Pirates

1979 Lou Brock, St. Louis Cardinals

1980 George Brett, Kansas City Royals

1981 Johnny Bench, Cincinnati Reds

1982 Andre Thornton, Cleveland Indians

1983 Ray Knight, Houston Astros

1984 Don Robinson, Pittsburgh Pirates

1985 Rick Reuschel, Pittsburgh Pirates

1986 Dennis Leonard, Kansas City Royals

1987 Paul Molitor, Milwaukee Brewers

1988 Ron Oester, Cincinnati Reds

1989 Dave Dravecky, San Francisco Giants

1990 Sid Bream, Pittsburgh Pirates

1991 Bill Wegman, Milwaukee Brewers

1992 Carney Lansford, Oakland Athletics

1993 John Olerud, Toronto Blue Jays

1994 Andre Dawson, Boston Red Sox

1995 Jim Abbott, California Angels

1996 Omar Vizquel, Cleveland Indians

1997 Eric Davis, Baltimore Orioles

1998 David Cone, New York Yankees

1999 Sean Casey, Cincinnati Reds

2000 Jason Giambi, Oakland Athletics

2001 Curt Shilling, Arizona Diamondbacks

2002 Tim Salmon, Anaheim Angels

2003 Jamie Moyer, Seattle Mariners

2004 Trevor Hoffman, San Diego Padres

2005 Craig Biggio, Houston Astros

2006 Mark Loretta, Boston Red Sox

2007 Mike Sweeney, Kansas City Royals

2008 Jon Lester, Boston Red Sox

2009 Mark Teahen, Kansas City Royals

2010 Tim Hudson, Atlanta Braves

CHAPTER NOTES

Chapter 1

1. Located in the middle of a plaza at Fifth and Vine in downtown Cincinnati and surrounded by office buildings, restaurants, shops, and hotels, the Tyler Davidson Fountain was given to the City by businessman Henry Probasco in honor of his deceased brother-in-law and business partner, Tyler Davidson. Officially titled "The Genius of Water," the 43 foot tall granite and bronze sculpture is topped by a nine foot statue of a lady with outstretched arms. Designed and made by Ferdinand von Miller and August von Kreling of Munich, Germany, the fountain was dedicated on October 6, 1871 in front of 20,000 people. The water that circulates in the fountain is turned off in the winter and turned back on every April to commemorate the first home game of the hometown Reds.

2. Ruether went 19–6 with an ERA of 1.82; Sallee, 21–7 and 2.06; and Eller, 19–9, 2.39. Eller also pitched a no-hitter in 1919. These three stalwarts were backed up by Ray Fisher (14–5, 2.17), Dolf Luque (10–3, 2.63), and Jimmy Ring (10–9, 2.26).

3. The White Sox finished the 1919 season with an 88–52 record and a 3½ game lead over second place Cleveland. Chicago had essentially the same ballclub that had won the A.L. pennant in 1917 and then defeated McGraw's Giants in the World Series in six games.

4. Initially, the White Sox were 8 to 5 favorites to win the Series. By the start of the Series the odds were even, and after the first game the odds changed to 5–7.

5. A former major league player and manager, Comiskey was an autocratic and penurious owner who treated his players like chattel.

6. The salaries of the White Sox were so low that they actually threatened to go on strike during the 1919 season, a fact gamblers would have noted with great interest. The ace of the White Sox pitching staff, Eddie Cicotte, played grudgingly for $5,500, about half of what his counterpart on the Reds, Dutch Reuther, made in 1919. Cicotte was also bitter that Comiskey had promised him a bonus of $10,000 if he won 30 games during the 1917 season, and then had Cicotte ride the bench after he had won his 29th game that season.

7. The ringleader of the conspiracy was first baseman Chick Gandil, who reportedly received $35,000 from gamblers behind the fix. Shortstop "Swede" Risberg received $15,000; pitcher Eddie Cicotte, $10,000 (although he was promised $20,000); and four others accepted the token amount of $5,000: pitcher Claude "Lefty" Williams, outfielder "Shoeless" Joe Jackson, outfielder Oscar "Happy" Felsch, and utility infielder Fred McMullin.

8. Morrie Rath, Cincinnati's second baseman, was the Reds' leadoff batter. Cicotte hit him in the back between the shoulder blades on the second pitch to him.

9. Cicotte was knocked out of Game One in the bottom of the fourth after giving up 5 runs in the inning. His delayed throw to second on an easy doubleplay ball which allowed the batter to beat the return throw to first and thereby extend the inning looked highly suspicious; as did the two-run triple he served up to the Reds pitcher Ruether.

The Reds won Game One 9–1; Game Two, 4–2; Game Four, 2–0; and Game Five 5–0. Chicago took Game Three 3–0.

10. Chicago won Game Six 5–4 and Game Seven 4–1 to cut Cincinnati's edge in games won to 4–3.

11. Williams was the scheduled pitcher for Game Eight. The thug who threatened him said that Williams not only had to make sure the Sox lost the game, he was not even to last one inning on the mound. Williams' record in 1919 was 23–11 with an ERA of 2.64.

12. Despite having an excellent curveball, Williams threw nothing but fastballs, 15 of them, in Game Eight. White Sox manager Kid Gleason took Williams out of the game in the first inning after he had allowed 4 hits and 3 runs; Williams was charged with a fourth run when a runner he put on base later scored off reliever Bill James.

13. Although the fix was practically common knowledge, the players, the gamblers, and Comiskey all wanted the hubbub over it to fade away. The players and gamblers were afraid of being prosecuted; Comiskey was afraid of losing his substantial investment in his players. Chicago sportswriter Hugh Fullerton did the most to keep the story alive and pressure reluctant authorities to investigate the matter.

14. Landis was the first commissioner of baseball, hired specifically to deal with the 1919 World Series. The trial, hampered by lost confessional documents, witnesses whose whereabouts could not be determined, and confusion caused by aliases used by gamblers, was a farce. The jury acquitted the players, but Landis ignored the verdict and brought down the hammer on the players. His famous verdict read in part: "Regardless of the verdict of juries, no player who throws a ball game, no player that undertakes or promises to throw a ball game, no player that sits in conference with a bunch of crooked players and gamblers where the ways and means of throwing a game are discussed and does not promptly tell his club about it, will ever play professional baseball." The reference to the "player that sits in conference" directly applied to third baseman Buck Weaver, who accepted no bribe but did not notify Comiskey of his knowledge of the plot. Weaver played honestly in the Series, but Landis, out to make an example out of him, banned him from the game as he did the players who accepted bribes.

15. The eight banned players ironically became more famous for being labeled members of the Black Sox than they would have been had they played honestly.

16. Babe Ruth, who was sold over the winter by the Boston Red Sox to the New York Yankees, is credited with saving baseball from itself. Overnight, he became the greatest hitter, most sensational personality, and biggest drawing card in baseball history. His 54 home runs in 1920 dwarfed anything ever done before in that department; he became an instant national hero; and his thrilling deeds turned around the public's souring attitude towards major league baseball.

17. Hutch's father would suffer a stroke in 1948 and retire. He died in 1951 at age 78. Hutch's mother died in 1962 at the age of 84.

18. Dorsett "Tubby" Graves coached college football and basketball at the University of Alabama, Texas A & M, and Montana State University (as the school is known today). He coached baseball at Alabama and Texas A & M, and at the University of Washington from 1923 through 1946. With University of Washington basketball coach Clarence "Hec" Edmundson he established the Washington State high school basketball tournament.

19. Though Bill was a successful surgeon, he eventually came to the conclusion "that the researcher, not the surgeon, would prevail in the struggle against cancer."

20. Bill said at the time, "I'm practically raising this kid."

21. Bill and John pitched tennis balls instead of harder baseballs to young Fred.

22. Fred's high school coach was named Ralph Reed.

23. Besides Detroit, Fred was scouted by the New York Yankees, Pittsburgh Pirates, Boston Red Sox, and Cleveland Indians.

24. DiMaggio played for his hometown San Francisco Seals and, foreshadowing his famous 56-game hitting streak for the Yankees, put together a 61-game hitting streak for the Seals in 1933 when he was only 19 years old.

25. Lelivelt was a longtime minor league outfielder who racked up 2,646 hits and a .332 lifetime batting average over an 18-season career that stretched from 1906 through 1931. He played in the major leagues for the Washington Senators (1909–1911), New York Yankees (1912–1913), and Cleveland Naps (1913–1914). Until 2007 Lelivelt held the International League record for the longest consecutive game hitting streak (42 games), which he set in 1912 with Rochester. His Seattle teams finished first in the P.C.L. in 1939, 1940, and 1941 and won pennants in 1940 and 1941.

26. Sicks Stadium was built at Rainier and McClellan Streets on the site of Dugdale Field, home of the former Seattle Indians. Dugdale Field, which burned to the ground, had been built in 1913. When it opened Sicks Stadium seated 15,000.

27. The Rainiers drew a league-best 437,161 fans in 1938. They had finished in sixth place the year before.

28. One sportswriter gushed about Fred: "He has control, a change of pace, a spiteful and unerring memory for batters' weaknesses, and an unholy desire to win." Another described him colorfully as "a precocious youngster with the build, memory and imagination of an elephant, and the imperturbable accuracy of a West Virginia squirrel gunner."

29. The players Detroit sent Seattle were: outfielder Jo Jo White, first baseman George Archie, infielder Tony Piet, and pitcher Ed Selway.

30. Hutch's brother John was responsible for putting the clause in the contract that ensured Hutch would share in any windfall enjoyed by the Rainiers for selling his services to a big league ballclub. Hutch attended the University of Washington for less than a semester in the fall of 1938.

Chapter 2

1. The Tigers had lost the 1934 World Series 4–3 to the St. Louis Cardinals and had won the 1935 World Series 4–2 over the Chicago Cubs.

2. The Tigers top starters were Tommy Bridges (17–7), Bobo Newsom (17–10), Schoolboy Rowe (10–12), Dizzy Trout (9–10), Al Benton (6–8), and Archie McKain (5–6). These six started 130 of the Tigers' 154 games.

3. At this point in the season Gehrig was 4–28 (.143), and all of his hits had been singles. The disease he was suffering from is called ALS or amyotrophic lateral sclerosis.

4. Babe Dahlgren is the player who replaced Gehrig. He batted .235 (15/89) for the season in 144 games.

5. The Yankees had five hitters who batted over .300 for the season: Joe DiMaggio, .381

(30/126); Charlie Keller, .334 (11/83); Red Rolfe, .329 (14/80); George Selkirk, .306 (21/101); and Bill Dickey, .302 (24/105).

6. Vernon Kennedy, Harry Eisenstat, and Jephat "Red" Lynn preceded Hutch on the mound; George Gill followed him.

7. Fred went all the way, giving up 10 hits, seven bases on balls, and three earned runs in eight innings. He struck out four and went 1–3 at bat. Attendance was only 2,500.

8. The win came in the second game of a DHer. Fred went 7.1 innings and gave up nine hits. All three runs scored against him were earned. Dizzy Trout got a save for 1.2 innings of scoreless relief.

9. This was Fred's best game of the season, as he held the Red Sox to six hits and Ted Williams to a 1–4 day. Even so, he walked seven. Hutch also had a big day at bat, going 4–4, scoring three runs, and knocking in two.

10. Fred lasted only 2.2 innings in this one. He gave up seven hits and five earned runs. His relievers didn't fare much better.

11. Fred finished with a 3–6 record and a 5.19 ERA. He gave up 95 hits and walked 51 in 85 innings.

12. The Tigers had finished in 4th place in 1938 with a record of 84–70. They slipped a bit to 5th in 1939 with a record of 81–73.

13. On May 4 at Philadelphia Fred gave up two home runs and five earned runs in 2.1 innings as the A's clubbed the Tigers 14–5. On May 9 at Boston Fred went five innings and surrendered nine hits and five earned runs. The Tigers lost 6–5 in ten innings, and Fred got a no-decision.

14. Fred's record with the Tigers for 1940 was 3–7 with a 5.68 ERA in 17 games. He gave up 85 hits in 76 innings, walked 26 and struck out 32. His three wins came July 24 versus Washington 7–5; August 3 versus Boston 6–4; and August 22 at Boston 9–8 in ten innings. His stellar performance came in the win at Boston when he pitched 8.1 innings of scoreless relief. Bobo Newsom started the game for Detroit but gave up two-run HRs to Joe Cronin and Bobby Doerr and was knocked out after allowing all eight runs Boston would score on the day in 1.2 innings. Fred gave up just four hits.

15. Detroit won Game 3 7–4; Cincinnati, Game 4 5–2. Both games were played in Detroit.

16. Fred pitched the bottom of the eighth inning and gave up one run, on a HR to pitcher Bucky Walters, who shut out Detroit on 5 hits 4–0.

17. Fred won 26 games for Buffalo, fashioned an ERA of 2.44, and was voted MVP of the International League. In 36 games he pitched 284 innings. He gave up 241 hits, walked 47, and struck out 171. Hutch also batted an amazing .392 (58–148).

18. Hutch was selected for the Army–Navy Game at the Polo Grounds on June 14, 1942; the Service All-Star team that played the A.L. All-Star team at Cleveland on July 7, 1942; and the 14th Naval District All-Star team in 1945.

19. Patsy was stationed in St. Augustine, Florida, as a member of the Women's Army Auxiliary Corp.

20. Hutch was based at Aiea Barracks in Hawaii. At the time of his discharge he had attained the rank of Lieutenant Commander.

21. The seven "good hurlers" named by Detroit sportswriter H.G. Salsinger were: Virgil Trucks, Rufe Gentry, Hal Newhouser, Dizzy Trout, Al Benton, Hal White, and Stubby Overmire. Ted Williams was also impressed, saying, "Detroit has the best pitching staff in the country, bar none."

22. On the year Trout went 17–13 with an ERA of 2.35; Trucks, 14–9 (3.23); Benton, 11–7 (3.64); and Newhouser, 26–9 (1.94).

23. Shortstop Johnny Pesky hit .335 and led the A.L. in hits with 208. Bobby Doerr hit .271 with 18 HRs and 116 RBI.

24. Ted Williams hit the tape-measure HR that landed high in the right field bleachers. The Red Sox painted the seat it hit red to commemorate the blast.

25. In the game of September 5, 1946, against Feller and the Indians Fred gave up only 5 hits, walked two, and struck out four. Fred improved to 10–11, while Feller's record dropped to 22–12. Fred finished the season with a 14–11 record, an ERA of 3.09, and 138 strikeouts in 184 innings. The strikeout total would be Hutch's season high for his major league career.

26. The other five Detroit "untouchables" were: Hal Newhouser, Dizzy Trout, George Kell, Dick Wakefield, and Hoot Evers.

27. The 4th inning brawl between the Yankees and the Tigers started when Billy Johnson, on first via a single, ran home on a double by Rizzuto and bowled over Detroit catcher Hal Wagner. Both Hutch and Houk were ejected from the game.

28. Speaking to a crowd of 200 high school boys, Hutch said, "It's sort of hard to explain and I wouldn't want you boys to think that it's the way to behave at a ball game. Honestly, though, I don't know how I got in there. My mind went blank. I guess it was kind of amnesia. You young ball players know better than to get in fights. Don't take me as an example."

29. The Yankees hit only five balls out of the infield all day against Hutch. Hutch didn't walk anybody and faced only 28 batters, since Joe DiMaggio, on base with one of the two hits given up by Fred, was erased on a double play in the second inning. The only other hit against Hutch came in the seventh on a bunt by Snuffy Stirnweiss. The Yankees' 19th consecutive wins had tied them with the 1906 White Sox. With three hits himself in the game, Fred out hit the Yankees.

30. The Tigers finished 85–69, in second place, 12 games behind the Yankees, who went 97–57. 1947 was the first year since 1939 that the Tigers did not have at least one 20-game winner.

31. Newhouser went 17–17 in 1947. He had won 80 games in the previous three years.

32. The game was played May 25 and Detroit lost 16–5. Hutch gave up six hits and five runs in two innings.

33. Fred replaced Johnny Murphy who became a scout for the Red Sox.

34. The Tigers finished 78–76, 18.5 games behind the pennant-winning Indians. Cleveland beat out Boston by one game and the Yankees by two and a half.

35. The new GM, Billy Evans, wouldn't agree to a pay raise for Hutch, so Fred signed for the same salary he earned in 1948: $18,000.

36. Concerning his infamous temper, Hutch said, "I take it out on inanimate objects. I don't get mad at my friends or family." Speaking of the destruction often left in Hutch's wake, Yogi Berra of the New York Yankees said, "If we got stools in the clubhouse, I knew he'd won. Otherwise we got kindling." Later, after Hutch had stated managing in the National League, Philadelphia sportswriter Larry Merchant said, "Hutch doesn't throw furniture. He throws rooms."

37. The five propositions presented by Hutchinson and Walker were: permission for the players to take their wives to spring training; the installation of warning tracks in the outfields of all major league ballparks; the establishment of minimum standards for lighting in all ballparks; requiring uniformity in the pitching mounds in all ballparks; and the installation of bullpen mounds in all ballparks.

38. The Tigers compiled a record of 87–67. They came in 10 games behind the 97–57 Yankees, who edged Boston by one game to take the pennant.

39. Hutch was ejected for arguing with umpire Art Passarella and had to be restrained by Rolfe and George Kell.

40. Fred's 8–2 win over Philadelphia on September 21 tied Detroit with New York. Hutch won four of five decisions in September.

41. Hutch had several arguments with plate umpire Ed Hurley, and after Hurley threw him out of the game he became so violent it took 5 players to restrain him.

42. The Tigers' 73–81 record in 1951 was the same as the mark recorded by the 1942 Tigers.

43. The Tigers were shut out three times and were batting .207 as a team.

44. The story about impending mutiny broke in Cleveland. Lyall Smith wrote a column entitled "Tigers Are Fighting Mad—at Manager Red Rolfe."

45. The statement Hutch released read as follows: "We feel it is unfair for Manager Red Rolfe to be blamed for our poor showing. He is a good manager. He has been wonderful to all of us while we have suffered all this bad luck at the start of the season. We want to refute that story from Cleveland. If there is any blame for our showing, the players themselves are accepting it. We are for Rolfe all the way."

Asked for a response to the statement, Rolfe said, "It was a fine gesture by the players. I deeply appreciate it. It is too bad the whole thing had to happen. But when things go bad, that's the way it is."

46. Rolfe went home to Gilford, New Hampshire, and in 1954 became the athletic director at Dartmouth, his alma mater.

Chapter 3

1. Fred Received a boost in pay from $20,000 to $30,000. He told the press, "We aren't a cellar team."

2. The skepticism was directed not at Hutch personally but at his past as a pitcher; a position considered incompatible with managerial success.

3. The move made room on the roster for catcher Matt Batts.

4. Dropo started the streak with a 5–5 day at Yankee Stadium on July 14. All five hits were singles: four off starter Jim McDonald and one off reliever Bob Hogue. The next day the Tigers played a doubleheader in Washington at Griffith Stadium. Dropo went 4–4 in the first game, again getting all singles, all off Walt Masterson. In his first at bat in the second game Dropo finally got an extra-base hit, a triple off Bob Porterfield, for hit #10. He singled in the third off Porterfield, and tied the record of 12 consecutive hits held by Boston's Pinky Higgins with a double off Lou Sleater in the fifth. The "Moose" remained tied with Higgins though when he faced Sleater again in the seventh and fouled out to the catcher. Dropo got one more hit in the game to go 13–14 in the three games, and after he went 2–4 the following day he set a major league record for the most hits (15) in four consecutive games.

5. Hutch was thrown out in the sixth inning of the first game of a doubleheader against the White Sox for arguing an out call at first base on Fred Hatfield.

6. In addition to Wertz, the Tigers gave up P Marlin Stuart, OF Don Lenhardt, and P Dick Littlefield. In return they got OF Jim Delsing, P Dave Madison, and P Bud Black from St. Louis, along

with Garver. Hutch's comment on the deal was "We've got a rebuilding job on our hands, and I think the new players will give us a lift."

7. Kuenn got a signing bonus of $55,000.

8. Spike Briggs' comment after signing Hutch to manage in 1953 was "We are pleased with the improved spirit Hutchinson has inspired in the players and are happy that he has agreed to continue as manager."

9. Newhouser beat St. Louis 3–2 in Detroit before a paid attendance of 526.

10. The season ended with a 8–2 loss to Cleveland at Tiger Stadium. Despite the poor season the players held a farewell party in the clubhouse.

11. Hutch laid down two rules: (1) No friends or kids in the clubhouse, and (2) Players not in the lineup are to pay strict attention to the game.

12. It was rumored that Garver had a sore arm when he came to the Tigers. On Opening Day he hurt his knee running to first on a double play groundball, and for some time his knee would partially pop out of the socket once or twice a game. He lasted two innings on Opening Day, surrendering five hits and four runs.

13. The 13 straight losses tied a club record. A 6–3 win over Boston in Detroit on June 8 allowed Hutch's club to avoid setting a new record.

14. The trade sent P Art Houtteman, C Joe Ginsberg, P Bill Wight, and INF Owen Friend to Cleveland; while pitchers Al Aber, Steve Gromek, and Dick Weik came to Detroit along with Boone. Hutch inserted Boone into the third spot in the batting order, and Boone responded with a fine season. He hit four grand slams on the year and finished the season batting .312 with 22 HRs and 93 RBI.

15. Kaline also showed off a great arm, throwing out several players who tried to run on him. He even threw out Cleveland's Dale Mitchell at second from a sitting position. About him Hutch said, "That kid will be a great hitter some day. He'll have good power, too."

16. Billy Hoeft (7–7) held New York to three hits in a 5–1 win in Detroit.

17. Hutch activated himself because his bullpen had become depleted. The starting rotation at this point consisted of Ralph Branca, Steve Gromek, Ted Gray, Ned Garver, and Billy Hoeft. Hutch pitched a total of 9⅔ innings in his final three appearances with no decisions. He ended his career as a major league pitcher with a 95–71 record in 242 games. He pitched 81 complete games, threw 13 shutouts, and compiled a 3.73 ERA.

18. The Tigers' 5–2 win at St. Louis on September 6 was their 51st win which surpassed the team's win total for 1952.

19. Detroit's final record for 1953 was 60–94; not good but a 10-game improvement over the previous year.

20. Hutch tied coach Heinie Manush for low score at the Early Wynn Invitational in Venice, Florida, on January 17.

21. Hutch was already annoyed about HBPs in spring training games, as Harvey Kuenn had been hit in the left hand by Karl Dews of the Phillies two days before the Yankee incident. New York's Harry Byrd hit Kuenn on the left wrist, which caused Kuenn to fall and sprain his right wrist. He was held out of competition for a week. Hutch's complete warning was "The Yankees have always been a fine club ... but if Byrd hits our fellows in the regular season we are going to strike back. We'll retaliate by pitching at their batters. That means Yogi Berra and all the rest."

22. About Zuverink, whom Detroit picked up from Cincinnati for $15,000, Hutch said, "You find

many cases like that in baseball. Zuverink never had a real chance. We were able to offer him one and he took advantage of it. By working regularly, his control improved. Control is still the big part of the pitching secret."

23. After Kuenn went through a 0–20 slump, he was batting .258. Hutch wasn't worried about him. "I never saw anyone hit in more tough luck. ... He'll be all right if he keeps hitting that ball sharply," said Hutch. For the second year in a row Kuenn became the first A.L. batter to collect 200 hits (#200 came on a single against Baltimore on September 22), which made him the first Tiger ever to collect 200 hits a year his first two years in the major leagues. He batted .306 on the year. Boone batted .295 (20/84); Dropo, .281; Kaline, .276; and Tuttle, .266. Gromek finished 18–16 with an ERA of 2.77; Garver, 14–11 (2.78); and Zuverink, 9–13 (3.64).

24. Seattle's GM was Dewey Soriano, Fred's old pitching teammate at Seattle's Franklin High School.

25. Hutch's contract reportedly made him the highest paid manager in the minors.

26. San Francisco was managed by Tommy Heath; Sacramento by Tony Freitas; San Diego by Bob Elliott; Los Angeles by Bill Sweeney; and Portland by Clay Hopper.

27. Seattle conducted spring training in Palm Springs. Two dozen players from the 1954 were gone, and the Rainiers had a total of 52 players in camp. In sizing up the competition Hutch said, "The Coast League may be faster than I thought it would be." On March 7 Hutch visited the Cleveland camp looking for players to purchase. Cleveland GM Hank Greenberg said, "No soap," in reference to his desire to sell.

28. Hutch fined two players (pitcher John Oldham and outfielder Carmen Mauro) $10 each for base running blunders. Most of the fines were $1 or $2 assessments, and the money collected went towards a post–season party. Hutch even fined himself $5, posting the bill on a blackboard in the clubhouse. He declined to disclose the nature of his infraction.

29. The award came with $1,500, which was split up among the players.

30. Total attendance was 387,205; paid attendance, 342,101.

31. The highest batting averages were turned in by Mauro (.293), Joe Ginsberg (.293), and Bobby Balcena (.291).

32. When Hutchinson was hired by the Cardinals, one of his best pitchers in Seattle, Bill Kennedy, offered this assessment of his former manager: "Hutch is a gambler. He always had our guys hitting behind the runner and it worked, although as a team we were slow. Although he was a good pitcher himself, he doesn't try to make you pitch his way. Let everyone pitch the way that is best for him, is his motto."

At his home on Anna Maria Island, Florida, Hutch revealed his basic managerial philosophy. "I feel a ballplayer is a man," he said. "I consider and treat him as such. I remember I was a player not too long ago. I made my mistakes and try not to lose sight of that fact." He stated that he would have two rules for the Cardinals: (1) produce on the field, and (2) don't corrupt the youngsters. He also had a rhetorical answer for those who again questioned whether he could be a successful manager given his background as a pitcher. "What do people think I did with my time in the three out of four games I was not pitching? Do they think I just sat in the bull pen reading comic books?"

33. Hutch's coaches were holdovers Bill Posedel and Terry Moore and new hire Johnny Hopp. Posedel and Moore filled Hutch in about the Cardinals' personnel. Hutch later refused to repeat their assessments to the press.

34. Mizell threw a 2-hitter with 13 strikeouts to lead Havana to a 9–0 win over Marianao.

35. *The Sporting News* reported during spring training that Hutch "has been very careful to give everybody a shot at a place on the club." When some of the Cardinals players visited Lakeland, Tigers players asked solicitously about Hutch.

36. At the end of April the Cardinals were in first place, for the first time since May 22, 1954.

37. Lane seemed to trade baseball players as casually as school boys swapping baseball cards. On May 11 he sent pitchers Harvey Haddix, Ben Flowers, and Stu Miller to the Phillies for pitchers Herm Wehmeier and Murray Dickson. On May 14 he swapped INF Solly Hemus for Philadelphia's Bobby Morgan (INF), and on May 16 he sent SS Alex Grammas and OF Joe Frazier to Cincinnati for INF Chuck Harmon. On May 17 he traded OF and 1955 N.L. Rookie of the Year Bill Virdon to Pittsburgh in return for OF Bobby Del Greco and P Dick Littlefield.

After being traded Hemus said, "I'll say this—and now that I'm going it might mean something— Hutchinson is about the best-liked manager I ever played for and his personality is paying off."

38. The deal sent Schoendienst, C Bill Sarni, OF Jackie Brandt, and Littlefield to the Giants; and SS Alvin Dark, 1B Whitey Lockman, C Ray Katt, and P Don Liddle to the Cardinals. The six players left on the Cardinals from 1955 were Stan Musial, Ken Boyer, Wally Moon, Rip Repulski, Larry Jackson, and Tom Poholsky.

39. In a 4–1 win over the Reds in St. Louis, a fan interfered with a drive hit by Bobby Del Greco. Although it was called a ground rule double, Hutch thought it should have been ruled a home run.

40. The play came during an 11–8 Cardinals win August 3 at Ebbets Field. The game ended an 8-game winning streak by Clem Labine over St. Louis. With the game tied 6–6 in the bottom of the 8th inning, Jackie Robinson hit a ground ball to Boyer at third. Two runs scored when it hit something and bounced over Boyer's glove. Hutch was able to grin about the stunt later since the Cards won the ballgame. On the other hand, on August 6 after an extra-inning 7–6 loss at Crosley Field, Hutch beat on the clubhouse walls, bruising his right hand and cutting the knuckles on his left hand.

41. The Cardinals' final record of 76–78 was an 8-game improvement over 1955. St. Louis finished behind Brooklyn, Milwaukee, and Cincinnati, 17 games out of first place.

42. Of all the countries visited by the contingent of volunteers, Fred was most impressed by Italy as a nation likely to adopt baseball as a leading national sport.

43. The dinner was held in honor of Stan Musial. It was a "black tie" affair, but Hutch showed up wearing a knit black tie and a light-colored suit. He was the only man at the head table not dressed in a tuxedo, but the considerate Garagiola tried to spare Hutch embarrassment by explaining to the crowd that it would have been impractical for Fred to wear a tux since he was in the midst of a whirl-wind tour, taking him from Florida to New York (to obtain his passport) to St. Louis and finally, imme-diately after the banquet, on to Europe for the series of baseball clinics. It was also Garagiola who said, "Hutch laughs. The only trouble is his face doesn't know it."

44. Hutch also said: "We'll not concede anything to anyone at present, and we'll make every effort to win it. There's no substitute for first place."

45. Mizell apparently lost his fastball during spring training, and a worried Hutch moved him to the bullpen.

46. The former holder of the N.L. record for consecutive games played with 822 was Gus Suhr. Musial set the record on June 12.

47. Hutch was criticized for letting Mizell, a lefty, pitch to Hodges, a right handed power hitter.

Hutch said: "It's my judgment that Mizell has enough stuff to get out right handers as well as left handers, and I happen to believe it's important to get him over the hump. If we're going to come close to winning the pennant, we're going to need help from him." By showing Mizell movies of his delivery, Hutch proved to him that his windup was exaggerated, causing him not to step directly enough towards home plate.

48. The Cardinals lost three to the Cubs and three to the Braves at home and then three to the Cubs in Chicago. They scored 13 runs in the nine games.

49. Hutch's complete statement was "I don't tell my pitchers to deliberately throw at any hitter. But what they do on the mound is their own business. These close pitches are part of the game. It's just that some of them get away from the pitcher."

50. The argument started when second baseman Don Blasingame, fielding a grounder hit by Dale Long, was bumped by Cubs runner Chuck Tanner, and no interference was called. Hutch was fined $50, and the N.L. did discipline Baker as well.

51. The vets Hutch allowed to go home early were: Stan Musial, Alvin Dark, Del Ennis, Wally Moon, Billy Muffett, Hobie Landrith, Herm Wehmeier, and Von McDaniel.

Chapter 4

1. Hutch told the press about his intention to hold Musial out of the game so they could inform Chicago fans, who might come to the game just to see the historic event, about his plans.

2. Jones went only 14–13 but turned in a sparkling 2.88 ERA, the best on the team by far; Mizell's 3.41 was the next best ERA. Jones' league-leading strikeout total was 225.

3. Wally Moon hit .238 with seven HR and 38 RBI. Del Ennis hit .261 but his total of 3 HR and 47 RBI was a major disappointment. The Cardinals also got little offense from the catching position. Hal Smith in 77 games hit .227 (1/24), while Hobie Landrith hit .215 (3/13) in 70 games.

4. Stan Hack finished the season at the helm and guided the team to a 3–7 record

5. *The Sporting News* reported that Hutch was also offered part ownership of the club, but apparently nothing came of this offer.

6. Hutch had not been a player on the 1934 Tigers, of course, but he was invited to the celebration as having been one of the managers of the ballclub since that year.

7. Hutch's contract was to run through the 1960 season.

8. Hook was 10–7 with 106 strikeouts and a 2.96 ERA in 140 innings when he was called up to Cincinnati.

9. McMillan broke his collar bone on August 11 in a game against Milwaukee.

10. The Reds lost 27 games in which they'd held the lead after the sixth inning.

11. Martin didn't know that Hutch was already wearing the number "1" and asked if the number were available for him to wear on his jersey.

12. Temple was an All-Star who'd hit .300 three times. The Reds traded him at the right time, as he never performed at an All-Star level again.

13. *The Long Season* also hit the best sellers list ... a rare accomplishment for a baseball book at the time ... and it has become a classic of the genre; along with Brosnan's follow-up, *Pennant Race*, his diary of the Reds 1961 season.

14. Hutch originally planned to install Frank Thomas at first base, thus freeing Robinson to play left field, but Thomas had a disappointing year. He hit .225 with 12 HR, and played 64 games at third, 33 in the outfield, and only 14 at first base.

15. McMillan suffered a broken nose in spring training but was ready to go when the bell rang. The three-run HR on Opening Day from the banjo-hitting shortstop came as a bit of a surprise, as he hit 68 HR in 6,752 major league at bats. Jim Brosnan was also a surprise as the Opening Day starting pitcher, and he lasted only 1⅔ innings, surrendering four earned runs on four hits and three walks. In a reversal of future roles, Jim O'Toole relieved Brosnan and pitched brilliantly, allowing only two hits over six innings. The official scorer gave O'Toole credit for the Reds' victory, but N.L. president Warren Giles later changed the decision and awarded the win to Brooks Lawrence.

16. McLish, whose full name was Calvin Coolidge Julius Caesar Tuskahoma McLish, was a finesse pitcher who relied as much on a knowledge of the hitter's weaknesses and tendencies as his own stuff. He had spent most of his career in the A.L. with Cleveland and had difficulty adjusting to the N.L.

17. Vada Pinson was the Reds batter whose BP line drive struck the boy.

18. Roberto Clemente's first inning grand slam off Don Newcombe gave the Pirates a lead they never relinquished.

19. Danny McDevitt and Ed Roebuck brushed Pinson back; Williams hit him on the arm in the seventh inning.

20. In one inning of work Sanchez walked two, hit three, and gave up two hits and four runs. He plunked third baseman Ted Lepcio, catcher Cal Neeman, and pitcher Gene Conley. The Reds released Sanchez four days after the fiasco against Philadelphia.

21. The loss in the second game of a doubleheader on June 5 was the Reds' seventh in their last eighth.

22. Slugger Joe Adcock beat out a bunt for a base hit.

23. Ed Mathews laid down a sacrifice bunt, which Joe Nuxhall fielded and threw over the first baseman's head.

24. The Reds acquired outfielders Wally Post and Harry Anderson and INF Fred Hopke for out-fielders Tony Gonzalez and Lee Walls.

25. Newcombe wanted to see the Floyd Patterson–Ingemar Johansson heavyweight fight on closed-circuit TV at a theatre in downtown Cincinnati.

26. When called up to Cincinnati, Coleman was hitting .324 (10/60) for Seattle. After his first meeting with Hutch, Coleman commented: "If you put this guy in a cage with a bear, you'd have to bet on him, not the bear."

27. *The Sporting News* reported that the extra BP was specifically for Ed Bailey, Jerry Lynch, Dutch Dotterer, Gus Bell, Willie Jones, Billy Martin, and Harry Anderson.

28. Drysdale was a nemesis of Cincinnati, and he threw at Reds' hitters frequently, especially Frank Robinson.

29. Martin was also fined $500 by Giles. Martin was sensitive to brush back pitches, as the year before he'd been hit in the face by a pitch from Washington's Tex Clevenger and hospitalized for 16 days. After the tight pitch from Brewer, Martin swung at a subsequent pitch and let the bat fly out of his hands towards the mound. According to Martin, Brewer said, "Do you want to fight?" Martin replied, "I'm just out here to get my bat, kid." Martin said he then hit Brewer with a preemptive punch

because he sensed that Brewer was about to punch him. The Cubs and Brewer later sued Martin for $1,040,000. Martin was served on August 22 at Wrigley Field when he left the batting cage because a Cubs official told him someone wanted to see him in the dugout. Martin's response to the suit was vintage Billy: "How do they want it? Cash or check?" Hutch was upset at the location and timing of the action, calling it a "bush league trick."

30. After the game, Mathews expressed admiration for Robinson's courage and resilience.

31. Robinson hit .341 (74–217) in the second half with 18 HR. While heel, ankle, and thumb injuries slowed him down, he still won the N.L. slugging title with a percentage of .591.

32. Pinson did lead the N.L. in doubles with 37.

33. DeWitt had previous front office experience with five other M.L. teams, most recently with the Detroit Tigers. With his brother Charles he had co-owned the St Louis Browns until they sold out to Bill Veeck. Bill eventually bought the Reds (for $4,625,000), although there was some controversy for a time related to the details of the sale of the team to him.

34. McLish pitched better in the second half of the year, but his 4–14 season record and 4.11 ERA was a major disappointment.

Chapter 5

1. This was the first Hot Stove League caravan in Reds history, and Hutch and DeWitt visited Lexington and Louisville, Kentucky; Richmond, Indiana; Huntington and Parkersburg, West Virginia; and Dayton, Lancaster, and Portsmouth, Ohio.

2. Hutch wanted the team to be tougher, mentally and physically. "Aggressiveness is hard to define. But you know when you've got it and when you don't have it. We didn't have it in 1960," he said.

3. Only eight writers predicted the Reds would finish in the first division (as high as fourth place), and seven of the eight predicted a fourth place finish. The other writer predicted a second place finish. Obviously, no one thought the Reds would win the pennant.

4. Hunt was a big kid … 6'4", 200 lbs. … and the star of training camp. He reminded Gabe Paul of former Reds ace Paul Derringer.

5. Cardenas was a skinny Cuban kid who displayed surprising power. Coach Reggie Otero took him under his wing and preached staying ready for his opportunities whenever they would come. On May 28 Cardenas was reduced to tears by a letter stating that his newly-purchased Cuban home and all the furniture in it had been confiscated by the Castro government.

6. The Reds lost 2–1, 5–3, 1–0, and 5–1 in the games of April 20–23.

7. The Reds were also excellent in close games and would finish 34–14 in one-run contests.

8. Also in reference to Hutchinson, Jay said, "In Milwaukee I felt like a statistic. Here they treat me like a human being."

9. Smith told *The Sporting News* that although Hutch was one of his dearest friends, the tongue lashing Hutch had administered to him in Los Angeles, full of the vilest epithets, was the worst he had ever endured, and made Smith want to punch Hutch.

10. In the sixth inning Robinson crashed into the left field scoreboard as he caught Tony Gonzalez's long drive, and in the eighth he made a diving catch on a sinking line drive hit by Clay Dalrymple.

11. With the Reds losing 6–4 with two out and two on in the seventh inning, Gus Bell singled, Gordy Coleman singled, Edwards walked, and Jerry Lynch drove them all in with a triple.

12. The Cubs beat the Reds 16–5, 7–2, and 15–8, outscoring them 38–15.

13. Robinson thought Coleman's omission was particularly egregious and asked if the voters had even looked at Gordy's stats and compared them to those of the other first basemen in the league.

14. The "Rally 'Round the Reds" song was written by Ruth Lyons, host of a Cincinnati TV variety show. Another song, "Root the Reds Home," was made popular by Rosemary Moore, and still another became current as the Reds marched towards the pennant.

15. Former bonus baby Jay Hook was affected half the season by a bad case of mumps in the spring, and Hunt gradually lost his ability to get hitters out. He finished the year 9–10 (3.97) and never pitched in the M.L. again.

16. Purkey beat Larry Sherry 6–0 and O'Toole beat Johnny Podres 8–0. Freese hit HRs #21 and 22 in support of O'Toole. The Reds were never out of first place again after the doubleheader sweep on August 16.

17. The double shutout against the Brooklyn Dodgers in 1935 was turned in by the New York Giants' Carl Hubbell and Clydell "Slick" Castleman. Hubbell was a Hall of Fame pitcher; Castleman from Donelson, Tennessee, had a six-year career in the majors, all with the Giants, and finished with a 36–26 record.

18. Orlando Cepeda and Felipe Alou homered off Jay; Jim Davenport off Jim Brosnan; and Willie Mays and Johnny Orsino off Bill Henry to tie a M.L. record.

19. Hutch took Jim Turner and Reggie Otero with him to New York.

20. This was the first shutout of Johnson's M.L. career. He held the Phillies to four hits.

21. O'Toole went 4–0 with a 2.63 ERA in September. He allowed 32 hits in 41⅓ innings.

22. John Edwards homered in the sixth and Robinson in the seventh to set the stage for Lynch's heroics. Robinson's HR was only his second since August 26.

23. In Pittsburgh the Dodgers lost the second game of their doubleheader 8–0. The Reds lost their final two games on September 30 and October 1 in Pittsburgh and finished 93–61, four games ahead of L.A. Cincinnati held first place for 114 out of 174 days.

24. *The Sporting News* editorial stated: "The sound job of managing by Fred Hutchinson cannot be overlooked. Hutch is known in baseball for his patience and his refusal to panic. He needed both qualities in the early going when the Reds fell into a long losing streak. He needed them several times during the season when they staggered and seemed ready to crumble. Always his calmness, his own ability to keep things on an even keel led the Reds through the dark hours."

25. The Yankees finished 1961 with a record of 109–53, eighth games ahead of Detroit. They played a 162-game schedule because of American League expansion, while the National League played the final 154-game schedule.

The Yankees hit a total of 240 HR. In addition to the 115 hit by Maris and Mantle, four other players hit 20 or more: Skowron 28, Berra 22, Blanchard 21, and Howard 21.

Artist Scott Hannig noticed in a photo that appeared in *Sports Illustrated* that three Reds players had been at the record-setting game. He depicts them (Joey Jay, Darrell Johnson, and Jim O'Toole, sitting left to right) in his drawing.

26. Mantle took BP before the game but did so in obvious pain.

27. Hutch thought that the Maris HR was the turning point of the Series. After the Series he said: "It ruined a fine pitching performance by Bob Purkey. And, after the loss, we just couldn't seem to bounce back."

28. Ford retired after five innings because of an injured ankle.

29. Mantle singled in the fourth, but with blood seeping through his bandages and uniform, Houk pinch ran Hector Lopez for him.

30. Richardson led all batters with nine hits. He'd also collected the most hits (11) in the 1960 World Series.

31. Pinson and Robinson had one hit each through the first four games: Freese none. For the Series they batted .091, .200, and .063, respectively.

32. The Yankees out hit the Reds .255 to .206 and outscored them 27 to 13 runs. The ERA of the Yankee pitching staff was 1.60 compared to that of 4.91 for the Reds. Hutch's summary of the Yankees' triumph was stoical: "We were overwhelmed, but they're a good team and they can do that to you."

Chapter 6

1. Hutch attended Hot Stove league affairs in at least five different cities: Cincinnati, Seattle, San Diego, Philadelphia, and Sarasota. The one in Cincinnati on February 10 was the first dinner held by the Cincinnati chapter of the Baseball Writers Association of America.

2. Hutch told the audience in Cincinnati: "In spring training I had my doubts too. But they had to have eight teams in the league so we started. But talk is cheap. I'm glad the players didn't pay attention to it last year and I know they won't this year."

3. The Reds lost Jay Hook, Gus Bell, Elio Chacon, and Sherman Jones to the New York Mets; and Ken Johnson and Dick Gernert to the Houston Colt 45s.

4. Freese broke his ankle on March 5 in the Reds first intra-squad game of the spring. He had singled to right field and was trying to stretch it into a double. He started to slide but then changed his mind and tried to hold up, causing his spikes to get caught in the clay. His shout of "I broke my 'blankety-blank' ankle" was clearly heard by people on other diamonds. He had surgery that night to repair torn ligaments. Freese had been looking forward to having a big year, as he felt secure with a team for the first time in his career.

5. The phrase echoed what grammatically challenged Dodgers manager Charlie Dressen said about the Bums' New York rivals in 1951 when the Dodgers swept them in early August to take a 12½ game lead over them: "The Giants is dead."

6. Maloney conquered his wildness, was recalled on June 7, and became an outstanding major league pitcher. Hunt, on the other hand, was further demoted from San Diego to Macon, Georgia. Drabowsky never got into a groove with the Reds. He was traded to Kansas City on August 13 after compiling a 2–6 record with an ERA of 4.99. Ellis was a bonus baby who had gone 10–3 with a 1.89 ERA at Columbia (Sally League) in his professional debut the previous year.

7. The Reds lost Opening Day at Crosley Field 12–4 to the Phillies. Joey Jay lasted only 2⅓ innings. Bob Purkey pitched a complete game to win the first game ever at Dodger Stadium, and Wally Post sealed the 6–3 win with a three-run home run in the 7th inning. Eddie Kasko got the first

hit at Dodger Stadium, doubling on the second pitch of the game. The Reds followed this win with a 6–2 loss in the first night game ever at Dodger Stadium. Sandy Koufax pitched a 4-hitter, while Moe Drabowsky was knocked out after four innings.

8. The installment of Harper at third base was a typically gutsy move by Hutch, who was never afraid to give young players a chance. Harper was sent down to San Diego before the Reds–Giants game on April 15. During this trial with the Reds he played in six games and batted .174 (4–23). Harper became a regular in 1963, batting .260 with 10 home runs and 37 RBI.

9. The Reds won the April 24 game at Crosley Field 7–3. Drabowsky earned a save, and Pinson and Post both homered. The win evened Ellis' record at 1–1. His first start had come April 14 in San Francisco, a 13–6 loss. He lasted 2⅓ innings and gave up seven runs, but only three of them were earned, as the Reds committed six errors and allowed six unearned runs.

10. Robinson's slow start was due, at least in part, to a back injury he had suffered during the April 13–15 series in San Francisco when he crashed into the fence making a catch. He went 13–70 in April with seven RBI.

11. The Reds traded Cliff Cook and pitcher Bob Miller to the Mets for Zimmer. Zim was one of a string of major leaguers produced by Cincinnati's Western Hills High School.

12. Former Red Ken Johnson shut out Cincinnati 2–0, handing Purkey (7–1) his first loss of the season in the process. The game was played at Colt Stadium, a temporary ballpark used for three years until the Astrodome was completed.

13. Jay got plenty of help in the 5–0 win: from Zimmer (3–5), Blasingame (4–4), and Cardenas (a HR and a single).

14. Klippstein and Keough had been acquired from Washington on December 15, 1961, for catcher Bob Schmidt and pitcher Dave Stenhouse. Initially, Hutch used Klippstein as a reliever but eventually moved him into the starting rotation. Klippstein got Hutch's attention by picking up his first win in the 2nd game of the May 30 DHer in Milwaukee; holding the Braves scoreless over the final three frames of the 16-inning affair. Klippstein finished the season 7–6 with a 4.54 ERA. Keough got his chance filling in for Vada Pinson for a week after Pinson pulled a leg muscle. As of June 18 Keough was hitting .333 (18–54) in games he started. For the season he would hit .278 (7/27) in 111 games. When Pinson missed the game on May 31, it ended his consecutive game streak at 508, the 4th longest streak in Reds history.

15. The Reds won 12–8 and 12–11 in 13 innings. A 55-minute rain delay made the actual time passed nine hours and 40 minutes. Frank Robinson had a good day with a grand slam homer, six RBI, and eight runs. Marty Keough tied the nightcap with a home run, and two batters later Cardenas won it with a single.

16. Following precedent, Hutch filled out his roster with the players who received the most votes after the starters, which caused Frank Robinson to be left out. For the 2nd All-Star Game, played June 30 at Wrigley Field and won by the A.L. 9–4, Hutch was allowed to add a few extra players, and he named Robinson to the team. Robby went 0–3 in the game.

17. Wills entered the game as a pinch runner for Stan Musial in the 6th inning. He promptly stole second so easily catcher Earl Battey did not even attempt to throw him out. Wills scored when Dick Groat singled over second. In the 8th, he led off with a single. When Jim Davenport singled, Wills stopped at second, but when left fielder Rocky Colavito held the ball for a moment and then threw to second, Wills ran to third, avoiding Brooks Robinson's tag after Bobby Richardson's throw, with a

beautiful slide. Felipe Alou then fouled out to Leon Wagner in short right. Wills tagged up, ran home, and slid under John Romano's tag.

18. Nuxhall went 5–0 with an ERA of 2.45.

19. New York's wins on August 4 were the franchise's first ever against the Reds; the Reds having won all 8 of the previous meetings. This Mets team was woefully bad, finishing with a 40–120 record. Klippstein lasted only ⅔ of an inning (he gave up 6 runs, 4 earned) in the 1st game. Hutch said, "You'd have thought that we were the last place club and the Mets were contenders."

20. Jack Sanford had the best year of his career, going 24–7 with an ERA of 3.43. Don Drysdale led the N.L. in wins with 25 (he lost 9), IP with 314, and strikeouts with 237. Drysdale won the Cy Young Award in 1962; Sanford finished second; and Purkey and Billy Pierce of the Giants tied for 3rd.

21. Robinson led the N.L. in slugging percentage and set team records in doubles (51), runs (134), extra-base hits (92), and total bases.

22. The Reds record of 98–64 in 1962 was essentially the same winning percentage (.605) as they had posted (.604) when they won the 1961 N.L. pennant.

23. Hutch was one of the main speakers at the January 12 banquet of the Cincinnati chapter of the Baseball Writers of America Association. He called his returning pitching staff "the strongest and deepest I've ever had as a manager." With Purkey, Jay, O'Toole, Brosnan, Henry, Nuxhall, and Maloney as shoo-ins to make the team, there were only three anticipated openings for pitchers on the roster.

24. *The Sporting News* picked the Reds to repeat as N.L. champs, as did more than a quarter of the BWAA members polled (68 of 254).

25. Rose was a favorite of Hutchinson. It was Hutch who sped up Rose's arrival in the majors by suggesting that Rose skip a couple of levels in the lower minors. During the winter Hutch had said, "If I had any guts, I'd stick that kid at second base and forget about him." Rose got his break when coach Mike Ryba advised him to stick around for the rest of an "A" team spring training game instead of heading to the clubhouse. "The way this game is going, you never know what'll happen," said Ryba. Rose pinch ran for Wally Post in the 9th inning, stayed in the game, and batted twice when the game went into extra innings. He doubled both times and opened eyes.

26. Hutch also benched slumping OFer Tommy Harper (2–18) and third baseman Gene Freese (3–18). They also got back into the lineup on April 27. Harper got going with the bat, but Freese, still rusty from his near year-long layoff, did not; and he was demoted to San Diego on May 14. Hutch said, "I'll take him back in 5 minutes if he shows me he's swinging the bat again." After hitting 12 HRs for San Diego, Freese called DeWitt and Hutch, reminding them of Hutch's promise. The Reds brought Freese back to the big leagues on July 14, but he never regained the stroke he wielded in 1961.

27. On May 3 versus St. Louis Rose hit a triple and his 1st major league HR. Hutch said, "I just hope Rose doesn't get the idea he's supposed to hit like Robby." Rose finished with the 2nd highest batting average on the team (.273) and won the N.L. Rookie of the Year Award.

28. Purkey went 6–10 with a 3.55 ERA. He was limited to 21 starts.

29. Jay went 7–18 with an ERA of 4.29. In his 1st eight starts the Reds scored a total of eight runs and were shut out three times. Jay got his 1st win in relief, and his 1st win as a starter on June 1. He shut out the Dodgers on four hits to win 1–0.

30. The only .300 hitter on the club was Vada Pinson who finished at .317.

31. The Reds beat Milwaukee at Crosley Field 4–3. Little-used OFer Ken Walters drew the GWRBI

base on balls. The Reds had loaded the bases three other times before the 12th inning and scored only once. Pinson reached base five times and never scored. Hutch said about the game: "That had to be frustration at its greatest."

32. Cardenas batted .235 on the year.

33. Doug Harvey threw Hutch out of the game on July 14 in the 1st inning. Stan Landes ejected him in the 8th inning on July 30. Cards manager Johnny Keane said about the latter dismissal: "I never saw Hutch madder."

34. Nuxhall went 15–8 and led the team in ERA (2.61) and complete games (14). On August 20 he notched his 100th N.L. win with a 1–0 win over Houston. He also tossed a 4-hitter against Pittsburgh on August 4 and a 3-hitter against New York on September 3. Tsitouris went 12–8 with an ERA of 3.16. He had previously won a total of six games in the majors. Tsitouris did not get his 1st start of the season until June 9 when he 4-hit the Phillies. He also 2-hit the Colts on July 3 and the Cardinals on September 27 and fired 3-hitters against the Cubs on September 15 and the Cardinals on September 22. Maloney served notice on the N.L. with a 16-strikeout performance against Milwaukee on May 21. He also whiffed 8 Braves in a row in that game: Eddie Mathews in the 1st; Norm Larker, Frank Bolling, and Denis Menke in the 2nd; Del Crandall, Bob Hendley, and Mack Jones in the 3rd; and Lee Maye in the 4th. Hank Aaron eneded the string of Ks by grounding out. Maloney led the Reds in shutouts with six. The Reds previous record for strikeouts in a season had been set in 1901 by Noodles Hahn with 233.

35. Hutch said: "I hope Jim is around 15 more years and wins 20 or more each year. If he is and I still am managing, and I hope I am, I'll be a great manager on Jim's arm." Hutch also said he liked the Phillies ballclub, which turned out to lead the N.L. for most of the 1964 season.

36. Hutch said: "Nobody'll get Edwards (in a trade). If they do, it'll be over my dead body."

37. DeWitt said: "We hope that the treatment will prepare him for the spring training period and for the 1964 season."

38. At the time, radiation treatment was experimental, having been tried in England and Australia mostly. Starting January 9 Hutch received treatment daily (2 million volts) for a week and then rested for three weeks.

39. Pointing to his upper chest Hutch said: "The cancer is here. No surgery will be involved. At least that's what they tell me at this time. But I believe it may wind up in surgery." When asked about his spirits, he said: "Fine, I hope." He added that the doctors had "given me no reason not to be optimistic. You know you're not alone in it. Lots of others have gone through it. I think I can, too."

40. The trip was to Frankfort, Germany on February 3. The clinics were for the personnel of the USAFE (United States Air Force in Europe) and lasted five days.

41. Dr. Orliss Wildermuth said: "This is extremely gratifying. Normally, at this stage of treatment, we are happy if the tumor has stopped growing. In Hutch's case a survey of the area of involvement showed a definite regression of the tumor."

42. According to Wildermuth, "His lungs are clean. We are unable to determine the point of origination. We know that the tumor is in the upper right chest, extending into the neck, above the collarbone. There is still a deformity."

43. The Reds lost the game 6–3. Johnson gave up five hits and three ER in 8⅔ innings. Umbricht broke into the majors with Pittsburgh in 1959. He became an effective middle reliever with Houston, going 4–0 with a 2.01 ERA in 1962 and 4–3 with a 2.61 ERA in 1963. His career record was 9–5 with

an ERA of 3.06. Umbricht faced his fate with good humor and stoicism and was greatly admired by his teammates for his attitude. To honor him the Colts wore black arm bands on their jerseys in 1964, and his uniform number was the 1st to be retired in Colts–Astros history. After the victory on Opening Day, Johnson said, "I had an extra special reason for wanting to win this one."

44. The Reds had scheduled off days on April 14 & 15, so Hutch did not miss a game while he stayed in Seattle.

45. Hutch's public comment on the results of the examination was "The doctors said they were very pleased with the progress I have made and that I will not have to report for another examination until June."

46. Coleman slumped to .242 (5/27) in 49 games and eventually lost the 1st base job to Deron Johnson. A former Yankees farm hand, Johnson had made the Reds team out of spring training on the basis of his power and versatility: he was competent at 1B, 3B, and the OF. He'd hit the most HR (8) of any Reds player in spring training. He played 131 games at first base and hit .273 with 21 HR and 79 RBI.

47. The Phillies had solid pitching and a dangerous lineup. Their big bats belonged to OFer Johnny Callison (.274/31/104) and third baseman Dick Allen (.318/29/91).

48. The Reds put the game away with a big late-inning rally. Hutch's telegram said: "Spent most enjoyable, relaxing night after 10 p.m. Keep it up."

49. After winning both games, 5–2 and 4–2, the Reds remained in 3rd place, 3½ games behind Philadelphia. Purkey won his 5th game (against six losses) in the opener; O'Toole ran his record to 12–4 by winning the nightcap. O'Toole would finish with the best record among Reds pitchers, 17–7 with a 2.66 ERA.

50. The 500-pound cake was donated by a local bakery. Among the many gifts Hutch received were: a check from DeWitt, a color TV from the Reds players, a pool table from the local writers, and a clock-barometer from the Dodgers players. Patsy and all four of the kids were on hand; Jack (18) having flown in from Cedar Rapids where he'd been playing on a Reds farm team. This was the last game of Hutch's managerial career, a 4–1 loss as Sandy Koufax fired a 5-hitter at the Reds. The Reds were 60–49 at the time which gave Hutch a composite 446–375 (.543) record as a Reds skipper. His lifetime record as a major league manager was 830–827 (.501). Hutch was recognized by an editorial the next day in the *Cincinnati Post Times-Star*, which read:

> Just 5 years ago last Sunday Fred Hutchinson came to Cincinnati as manager of the Reds baseball team. He inherited a six-place team which he turned into a National League pennant winner in 1961.
>
> Hutch has just turned 45 and the gifts and kind words and cheers for him at Crosley Field last night were the sincere sentiments not only of the baseball fans at the game, but of the 4-state area which is Reds territory.
>
> The esteem and respect in which Hutch is held by owners, players and fans is something he has fully earned by his baseball knowledge, his courage and his overpowering desire to win. Every fan retains the right to "second guess" the head man, but most of the local "experts" admit that Hutch's strategy has been proved to be right most of the time.
>
> So we join in the singing of Happy Birthday to a man who as player and manager has always been a credit to baseball, to a man who is in every way a fine guy.

51. Ruiz ran on his own, flabbergasting third base coach Reggie Otero who wasn't able to verbalize a command not to try the play. Frank Robinson noticed Ruiz running and faked a bunt to distract the Philly catcher.

52. Nineteen year old Billy McCool was a pleasant surprise, who bolstered the Reds bullpen. He appeared in 40 games, three as a starter. He went 6–5, posting a 2.43 ERA.

53. At this point the Reds controlled their own destiny. All they had to do was win, but they lost four of their last five games.

54. McCool was a surprise starter, and he did a fine job, tossing a shutout until the 9th inning, when Bill Mazeroski singled in Bob Bailey and Roberto Clemente. The Reds got 11 hits off Bob Friend but couldn't score.

55. Catcher Jerry May squeezed home Donn Clendenon who had doubled to open the inning and been sacrificed to third by Mazeroski. Maloney went 11 innings, allowing three hits and no runs while striking out 13. Bob Veale went 12⅓ innings for Pittsburgh and struck out 16. The Reds left 18 runners on base. The loss put the Reds one game behind St. Louis.

56. The Reds won 5–4, scoring the winning run in the bottom of the 7th on Vada Pinson's triple and Frank Robinson's double. Reserve catcher Jim Coker had three hits, including a HR. Philadelphia squandered a 6½ game lead with two weeks to go by losing ten games in a row.

57. The Reds appeared to have the Phillies whipped until Leo Cardenas over–reacted to being hit by a Chris Short pitch in the 7th inning. Cardenas started to rush the mound, bat in hand, before he was intercepted by catcher Clay Dalrymple. The aroused Phillies scored four runs in the top of the 8th to win the game. Their rally was started on a catchable bloop hit by Frank Thomas which Cardenas appeared to petulantly give up on. Afterwards, pitcher Jim O'Toole and Cardenas got into it in the Reds clubhouse. After O'Toole pushed Cardenas down, Cardenas grabbed an ice pick; but before he could accost O'Toole with it, Joey Jay disarmed him, saying, "If there's gonna be any fighting, it won't be with an ice pick."

58. Jim Bunning held the Reds to six hits. Dick Allen hit a pair of HRs and drove in four runs.

59. The Reds refunded $1,400,000 worth of orders for World Series tickets.

60. Pete Rose was also on the bus, as he was playing Winter League ball for Otero. Rose had suffered a bit of the sophomore jinx in 1964 and was intent on improving his hitting and defense at second base. Rose, who was grateful for the shot at the big leagues that Hutch gave him, said repeatedly that one of his biggest disappointments in baseball was never having hit .300 in the major leagues for Fred Hutchinson.

Chapter 7

1. The *Cincinnati Post & Times-Star* of November 12, 1964, published testimonials to Hutch from several people. Gabe Paul said: "Hutch was a real man who had the strength of his convictions and was loyal and dedicated. One of the greatest experiences that I can look back to is having been associated with him."

Dick Sisler said: "This has cost baseball a great man and a great manager. I can't tell you how saddened I am. I think any sport which loses a great competitor like Fred has suffered a great loss. He was a grand guy."

President of the N.L. Warren Giles said: "He could have been best described as utterly indestructible. To use baseball language–one from the old school. A man whose rough surface covered a kindly and sentimental person. He made a great contribution to baseball and we can't afford to lose men like him."

Dr. J.H. Beam, Hutch's personal physician in Bradenton, Florida, who attended him the last week of his life, said: "He was a great guy. It is too bad. He said very little to me or anyone else. It was very hard. His family had been expecting it, but it was still very hard."

2. DeWitt's complete statement in the *Cincinnati Post Times-Star* was: "It was a tremendous personal loss because Hutch was one of my closest friends. Our relationship was employer-employee, but it was more on a man-to-man basis. He was nicknamed 'The Bear' because he was a terrific competitor and because of his gruff exterior. But, underneath it all, he was very soft-hearted, genteel, and one of the most loyal persons I've ever had the pleasure to know. He had many friends in and out of baseball. And I'm sure we'll all miss him and his wonderful personality. He was a very successful manager as our record of the past four years—the best in the league—shows."

3. The service was held at Roser Memorial Community Church. Honorary pall bearers were: Bill DeWitt, Dr. George Ballou, Hoot Evers, Hank Greenberg, Frank Slocum, Joe Garagiola, J.D. Webb, Jim King, Bill McKecknie Sr. and Jr., Benny Scanio, Bill Veeck, Dick Sisler, Jim Turner, and Reggie Otero.

4. Hutch was buried in Mt. Olivet Cemetery in Renton, Washington.

5. Hutch's #1 was the 1st number in Reds history to be retired.

6. The other members of the Class of 1965 for the Reds Hall of Fame were: Larry Kopf, Red Lucas, Wally Post, and Johnny Temple.

7. *Sport* named Hutch their 18th annual Man of the Year in their issue for February 1965. The Magazine's statement about Hutch on page 34 reads: "The world of sport is known, too, as the world of games, a world of meaningless accomplishment and activity when set in proper perspective. But sometimes the world of games is a setting for an act of courage which glitters with meaning when measured by any yardstick. And such an act of courage was evident in 1964. Fred Hutchinson, tortured by cancer, continued at his job, managing the Cincinnati Reds as long as physically possible. For his courage, for the shining example he set, *Sport's* highest honor."

Hutch won other honors long after his death. For example, in 2000 in a poll taken by the Seattle newspaper he was named the best athlete to ever come out of Seattle; and, according to *Redleg Journal* "At the end of each row at Safeco Field in Hutchinson's hometown of Seattle is a foot-tall cast-iron image of the former Reds manager."

8. The FHCRC evolved in this way: in 1956 Dr. Bill Hutchinson created the Pacific Northwest Research Foundation. In 1965 the Foundation created the Fred Hutchinson Cancer Center, and in 1975 the Fred Hutchinson Cancer Research Center became an independent entity.

9. The three Nobel Prize winners for physiology or medicine are: E. Donnall Thomas (1990, "for his pioneering work on bone marrow transplantation"); Lee Hartwell (2001, "for his discoveries or regulation of the cell cycle"); and Linda Buck (2004, "for her discoveries of odorant receptors and the organization of the olfactory system").

10. Prince, Enright, and Collett are routinely named as the three friends of Hutch who created the Hutch Award, but *Total Baseball* (8th ed.) says that two others were also involved: broadcaster Ernie Harwell and sportswriter Joe McGuff. According to *Total Baseball* Collett ran the business out of his home in Dayton, Ohio, until 1994, after which he turned the administration of the Award over to the Seattle Mariners major league baseball club in conjunction with the *Seattle Post-Intelligencer* and the Fred Hutchinson Cancer Research Center. Originally, voting for the Award was presumably done by the originators (the plaques themselves say "This award is made by the Baseball Writers of

America and the Major League Broadcasters ... all friends of 'Hutch'"), but eventually the voting was turned over to past recipients of the Award.

11. The Hutch Award itself has gone through three incarnations: the original metal plaque; an etched glass plaque; and the current award (first given away in 2006), a blue and yellow glass sculpture called "Cerulean Venetiar with Sun Yellow Coils" and made by artist Dale Chihuly. The original steel alloy plaque, bearing Hutch's image, weighs 19 pounds and measures 16" × 20" × ½". Over the years and by different sources, varying phrasing has been used to describe the qualifications for the Award. The original plaque recognizes the winner "as the baseball player most typifying the courage and character of Fred Hutchinson" and mentions four traits in particular: Honor, Courage, Dedication, and Manliness. However, "competitiveness" was definitely an integral part of Fred Hutchinson's character, so it is not surprising that "competitiveness" or "competitive spirit" has often been mentioned as a qualification for the Award. In addition, *Total Baseball* mentions that "consideration is given to players who overcome major physical adversity," and even a cursory study of the list of past winners shows that that trait certainly appears to have greatly affected past elections.

12. In his autobiography *The Mick*, Mantle says, "I've often thought that a lot of awards you get are made-up deals so you'll come to the dinner. Of course, there are awards that have merit. I won the first Fred Hutchinson Award. It's for courage. He was a pitcher, and later a manager in the majors. He had courage, but he never let us feel sorry for him. He made us feel good just because we knew him. I truly appreciate that award. It's one of my favorites."

13. The nine Hall of Famers are: Carl Yastrzemski, Al Kaline, Willie McCovey, Willie Stargell, Lou Brock, George Brett, Johnny Bench, Paul Molitor, and Andre Dawson.

14. Danny Thompson was a shortstop who was diagnosed with leukemia before the 1974 season. He kept playing baseball in the majors through 1976 and died about ten weeks after the '76 season at the age of 29.

15. On October 7, 1988 Dravecky, suffering from cancer, had surgery on his pitching arm which removed half of the deltoid muscle. He made a comeback to the majors in 1989, but halfway through his second game the humerus bone in his arm snapped. Later that summer while celebrating the Giants' pennant he broke the arm again. He underwent two more surgeries and finally had his left arm and shoulder amputated on June 18, 1991.

16. While at the University of Michigan Jim Abbott was named the Big Ten Athlete of the Year for 1988. He also won a gold medal at the 1988 Summer Olympics. He played for four major league teams, won a total of 87 games, and pitched a no-hitter against the Cleveland Indians,

17. Lester was scratched from his start against the Oakland Athletics on August 27, 2006 because of a sore back. In early September he was diagnosed with anaplastic large cell lymphoma.

18. Lester's first start in his return to the big leagues was on July 23, 2007, in Cleveland. He went six innings, allowing two runs, and got the win.

19. Lester's no-hitter was the 18th in Red Sox history. He threw 130 pitches, walked two, and struck out nine.

BIBLIOGRAPHY

Books

Anderson, William M., ed. *The View from the Dugout: The Journals of Red Rolfe: An Unparalleled Look Inside the Mind of a Major League Manager*. Ann Arbor, Michigan: The University of Michigan Press, 2006.

Anderson, William M. *The Detroit Tigers: A Pictorial Celebration of the Greatest Players and Moments in Tigers History*, fourth edition. Detroit, Michigan: Wayne State University Press, 2008.

Anton, Todd and Bill Nowlin, eds. *When Baseball Went to War*. Chicago: Triumph Books, 2008.

Asinof, Eliot. *Eight Men Out: The Black Sox and the 1919 World Series*. New York: Holt, Rinehart and Winston, 1963.

Brosnan, Jim. *The Long Season*. New York: Harper & Bros., 1960.

Brosnan, Jim. *Pennant Race*. New York: Harper & Bros., 1962.

Jordan, David M. *Tiger in His Time: Hal Newhouser and the Burden of Wartime Ball*. South Bend, Indiana: Diamond Communications, 1990.

Lawson, Earl. *Cincinnati Seasons: My 34 Years with the Reds*. South Bend, Indiana: Diamond Communications, 1987.

Marazzi, Rich and Len Fiorito. *Baseball Players of the 1950s: A Biographical Dictionary of All 1,560 Major Leaguers*. Jefferson, North Carolina: McFarland, 2004.

Overfield, Joseph M. *The 100 Seasons of Buffalo Baseball*. Kenmore, New York: Partners Press, 1985.

Pietrusza, David, Matthew Silverman, and Michael Gershman. *Baseball: The Biographical Encyclopedia*. Kingston, New York: Total/Sports Illustrated, 2000.

Rhodes, Greg and John Snyder. *Redleg Journal: Year by Year and Day by Day with the Cincinnati Reds Since 1866*. Cincinnati, Ohio: Road West Publishing, 2000.

Skipper, John C. *A Biographical Dictionary of Major League Baseball Managers*. Jefferson, North Carolina: McFarland, 2003.

Thorn, John et al. *Total Baseball: The Ultimate Baseball Encyclopedia*, 8th edition. Toronto, Ontario, Canada: Sports Media Publishing, 2004.

Waddingham, Gary. *The Seattle Rainiers 1938–1942*. Self-published, 1987.

Articles

Cohane, Tim. "Fred Hutchinson: Angry Boss of the Reds." *Look*, August 27, 1963, 66–69.

"Fred Hutchinson: Man of the Year." *Sport*, February 1965, 34–35.

Harmon, Pat. "Fred Hutchinson: Slow Man with the Hook." *Baseball Digest*, September 1961, 13–14.

Harmon, Pat. "Hutchinson, the Fighter." *Baseball Digest*, March 1964, 23–24.

"Mr. Hutch Is Rough in a Clutch." *Life*, October 6, 1961, 103–104.

O'Neil, Paul. "One Rookie They Won't Forget: Wonderboy Hutchinson." *Saturday Evening Post,* March 11, 1939, 35+.

Schmetzer, Mark. "Gus Bell Remembers How 'Hutch' Spurred '61 Reds to pennant." *Baseball Digest,* November 1986, 83–86.

Shaw, Dale. "Fred Hutchinson: The Manager Down the Stretch." *Sport*, November 1963, 52–64.

Smith, Lyall. "Control Champ: Hutchinson." *Baseball Digest*, June 1952, 11–12.

Newspapers

The Cincinnati Enquirer
The Cincinnati Post & Times-Star
The New York Times
The Sporting News

Websites

Baseball Almanac—www.baseballalmanac.com
Baseball Chronology—www.baseballchronology.com
Baseball Reference—www.baseballreference.com
Baseball in Wartime—www.baseballinwartime.com
Fred Hutchinson Cancer Research Center—www.fhcrc.org
Free Online Encyclopedia of Washington State History—www.historylink.org
Retrosheet—www.retrosheet.org

INDEX

INDEX